EMPOWERMENT SKILLS FOR LEADERS

A COMPONENT OF THE NATIONAL FAMILY DEVELOPMENT CREDENTIAL PROGRAM

Claire Forest, PhD

Katie Palmer-House, EdD

Carol West, M.A.

Copyeditor: Robert Kulik

Illustrator: Camille Doucet

Graphic Designer: Tina Field Howe

Third Edition

© 2020 Claire Forest

Forest Home Press LLC

A Word about Copyright

National FDC Director Claire Forest owns the copyright to all the National Family Development Credential Program publications, including *Empowerment Skills for Family Workers* and its accompanying *Instructors Manual* and *Portfolio Advisor Manual*, as well as *Empowerment Skills for Leaders* and its accompanying *Instructor Manual*, all FDC exams and protocols, and all forms used in the management of the Family Development Credential program and on the FDC website: www.familydevelopmentcredential.org.

A copyright protects an author (or program developer) from others claiming that original author's work as their own, or from inserting bits and pieces of that work into their own without permission or proper attribution. Thus, the copyright protects the original work from being represented. In the context of the current work, it helps ensure that people who earn the Family Development Worker's Credential or the Family Development Leadership Credential have studied the genuine and authentic course.

How do I share what I've learned?

If you want to share what you've learned, you have several options; for example, you could:

- Offer a short workshop. If you copy a handout, leave the copyright and source statements intact.
- Write an article, including short quotes from this book, with proper attribution, for example: "From Claire Forest, *Empowerment Skills for Leaders* (Forest Home Press, 2020)."
- When citing quotations, include the relevant page number(s).

Email Claire at cnd3@cornell.edu or Amy Knight at nationalfdc@uconn.edu with any questions that you have about using the curriculum.

Dedication

I honor my mentor, Professor Urie Bronfenbrenner (1917–2005), who co-founded the federal Head Start program in 1964. He then wrote a pair of groundbreaking publications which profoundly influenced child and family policy.[1]

In 1981, Professor Bronfenbrenner welcomed me as the Dissemination Director of the US branch of his five-nation, Cornell University *Ecology of Human Development* study, also known as "Family Matters." My mission within his vibrant wing of Cornell University's land grant College of Human Ecology was to forge "outreach" collaborations with community partners, to infuse these new approaches into policies and practices. My principal partners at local, state, and federal levels included Head Start, Cooperative Extension, Community Action, Child Care Councils, New York State Council on Children and Families, and eventually, the Family Development Credential Program (FDC)—founded 25 years ago—for which I serve as director.

After Professor Bronfenbrenner's eminent life neared the end, I was invited by Sara Harkness and Charles Super, professors at the University of Connecticut to move the National Family Development Credential Program to their land grant university. At UConn's Center for the Study of Culture, Health, and Human Development (CHHD) in the Department of Human Development & Family Studies, the seed I had planted under Professor Bronfenbrenner's guidance continued to grow.

The Office of Head Start established new Performance Standards Section 1302.91(e)(7) for Staff Qualifications and Competency, requiring all Head Start family workers to earn either a bachelor's degree or an approved credential. As a result, thousands of Head Start Family Workers have earned the Family Development Credential, a major step toward transforming the nation's way of working with families. Here at National FDC, we appreciate our continuing collaboration with National Head Start, offering Instructor Institutes at several Head Start conferences each year.

I appreciate my colleagues: Professors Harkness and Super, Lead Instructor Carol West, Program Manager Amy Knight, Instructor Sue Pappas, and our capable FDC State Coordinators and Instructors. I am grateful for the serendipity that led me as a young, green translational scholar (before we used that term) on this journey to help fulfill Professor Bronfenbrenner's prophetic goals, which continue to be my watchword. I hope they will be yours too. Workers cannot transform their ways of working unless agency leaders understand and embrace these strength-based principles. Welcome to *Empowerment Skills for Leaders!*

–Claire Forest, PhD

The responsibilities of the research extend beyond pure investigation, especially in a time of national crisis. Scientists in our field must be willing to draw on their knowledge and imagination in order to contribute to the design of social inventions: policies and strategies that can help to sustain and enhance our nation's most precious resources—the nation's children.[2]

–Urie Bronfenbrenner

---

[1] Urie Bronfenbrenner, "Beyond the Deficit Model in Child and Family Policy," *Teacher College Record* 81, no. 1 (1979a): 95-104; Urie Bronfenbrenner, *The Ecology of Human Development: Experiments by Nature and Design* (Cambridge, MA: Harvard University Press, 1979b).

[2] Urie Bronfenbrenner, ed., Making Human Beings Human: Biological Perspective of Human Development (Thousand Oaks, CA: Sage, 2005).

Acknowledgements

Once the FDC training curriculum and credentialing system was established, the natural next step in the process of transforming the way agencies work with families was to develop a leadership component. This component was prepared for family support supervisors and leaders to review and practice the critical skills needed to develop mutually respectful, empowerment-based relationships with staff members, collaborators, and community stakeholders.

There are many people to thank as we complete this update of the FDC leadership curriculum. We greatly appreciate the insights and suggestions from a group of experienced and talented FDC instructors who facilitate *Empowerment Skills for Leaders*. They are Rosalyn Ferguson, New York City; Haley Scott (Connecticut Office of Early Childhood, Hartford, CT); Caroline Mavridis (Center for the Study of Culture, Health & Human Development, University of Connecticut); Erica Henry (Washington, DC); Sonya Montoya (Flagstaff, AZ); and Angela Zimmerman (Molloy College, Long Island, NY). Angela and her team also compiled an extensive list of relevant articles to supplement the curriculum as additional resources.

A special thank you goes to Angela Zimmerman, Lisa Miller, and Sherry Radowitz (Molloy College) for pioneering the adaptation of *Empowerment Skills for Leaders* for the higher-education audience. While the curriculum was initially developed for leaders and supervisors in the human services field, Angela and her team recognized how beneficial it would be for leaders within the various departments of the college. To this end, they facilitated several cohorts of department leaders and college administrators—and with great success. In the summer of 2019, National FDC collaborated with Molloy College to hold its first Instructors Training Institute specifically for those in higher education, with representatives from several different colleges and universities participating.

It was a great pleasure to work with Camille Doucet, the skillful artist and illustrator of *Empowerment Skills for Family Workers*, who sketched the cover and text illustrations for the first edition of *Empowerment Skills for Leaders*. You will see her "peripheral vision" sketch in this updated edition.

We are also grateful to our former colleagues at the New York State College of Human Ecology and Cornell Cooperative Extension for the opportunity to collaborate in promoting the principles and practice of family development that foster healthy families and caring communities.

To our own families, we send our deepest thanks for your gifts of love, now and always. As you nurture and inspire us to realize our own empowerment potential, you teach us the meaning of love.

Claire, Katie, and Carol

About the Authors

Claire Forest, PhD

Claire is Assistant Professor in the University of Connecticut's Department of Human Development and Family Studies, where she directs the National Family Development Credential Program. In 2016, the Federal Office of Head Start approved the National Family Development Credential for fulfillment of requirements under section (1302,91 e) (7) of the Head Start Performance Standards, Staff Qualifications and Competency. Claire especially appreciated this recognition, as it represented the fulfillment of her mentor Urie Bronfenbrenner's vision.

Prior to moving to the University of Connecticut, Claire was a faculty member of Cornell University's Department of Human Development (1981–2010). She directed the Cornell Empowering Families Project, which developed and administered the Family Development Credential Program until 2010, when the program moved to the University of Connecticut. She has authored many publications, including the FDC curriculum— *Empowerment Skills for Family Workers*, the first edition of which was published in 1995. She also authored a 1995 monograph entitled *Credentialing Caregivers* and commissioned by the Harvard Family Research Project.

From 1981 to 1991, Claire served as Training and Dissemination Director of the Cornell Family Matters Project, overseeing national implementation. Before joining Cornell, Claire directed a day-care center and family resource center. She is widely respected as a leader in the field of family support and engagement.

Katie Palmer-House, EdD

Katie was Senior Trainer of the Cornell Empowering Families Project from 2000 to 2010. Before joining Cornell, she was an FDC instructor and portfolio advisor in Dutchess County, NY, and worked as a frontline family support supervisor and deputy director of a community action agency. During her years with National FDC, Katie made many important contributions, especially to *Empowerment Skills for Leaders*, including the section on learning styles, which is included in this edition. Her research focused on adult and community education, and teaching practices that foster transformative learning.

Carol West, M.A.

Carol joined the National FDC team in 2011 as the Senior Trainer and Portfolio Reviewer. Prior to her consulting work with FDC, Carol had a long career with Cornell University Cooperative Extension in Jefferson County, NY. During her tenure with Cooperative Extension, her educational focus included youth development, parenting education, child care, and family engagement.

Carol was also Director of a statewide Parental Information and Resource Center, the goal of which was to assist schools and community agencies to more effectively engage parents in their children's education. In addition, she was an instructor and portfolio advisor for both *Empowerment Skills for Family Workers* and *Empowerment Skills for Leaders*, teaching several classes over the years.

INTRODUCTION

Empowerment Skills for Leaders is a component of the comprehensive curriculum of the National Family Development Training and Credentialing (FDC) Program initially developed by the Cornell Empowering Families Project at Cornell University in the mid-1990s. Since 2010, the program has been administered by the University of Connecticut. The core component of the curriculum, *Empowerment Skills for Family Workers: A Worker Handbook*, was written by National FDC Director Claire Forest as part of a major New York State Initiative to develop a family-centered, strengths-based, professional development training program for frontline family workers.

Empowerment Skills for Leaders was initially developed for family support professionals interested in supervising and leading their organizations using the principles and practices of the Family Development approach. However, both curricula have expanded their audience to include professionals from a variety of different fields, including business and higher education.

How this program differs from other programs

Empowerment Skills for Leaders is a professional development training for supervisors and leaders interested in using empowerment-based leadership in their agencies, businesses, or educational institutions. Leaders who already have FDC credentialed staff in their organization will be able to enhance their organization's capacity for providing empowerment-based support using the same principles and practices that their family workers use with families. Leaders who are unfamiliar with FDC will learn practical ways to build their organizational capacities in areas of empowerment-based supervision, interagency collaboration, strengths-based assessment, multicultural competence, and personal self-empowerment.

Empowerment Skills for Leaders differs from traditional leadership development trainings in the following ways:

- It is designed to help leaders build on specific skills and competencies they already have, and that workers have learned through strengths-based family development training. Most leadership training programs provide information about ways to use generic strategies in all-purpose situations.

- *It provides an in-depth, interactive, and reflective program that encourages personal and organizational transformation.* Leadership trainings are often conducted in one-day, or time-intensive, large-group seminars with little or no time for open discussion or personal reflection.

- It was developed for all levels of leadership in organizations, from board members and executive directors to frontline supervisors. Most leadership programs are created for executive management or top administrators who then become responsible for implementing organizational change.

- It helps leaders identify the areas where empowerment-based change within the organization can begin to make meaningful differences in family support programs and agency-based outcomes. Most leadership programs focus on teaching motivational techniques designed to increase staff productivity without understanding that policies and practices of the organization may also need to change for families to accomplish goals, and for agencies to achieve outcomes.

- It promotes networking and collaboration among participants in a positive learning environment to support their collective goals. Most leadership programs focus on the individual and not as much on partnering with other professionals.

How Empowerment Skills for Leaders was developed

Empowerment Skills for Leaders (ESFL) was first published in 2002. It was developed over a year and a half, involving focus-group research with FDC-credentialed supervisors and other community leaders, as well as curriculum reviews and pilot testing of training activities. Many of the activities in this course were field tested in leadership pilot programs and found to be useful in starting or advancing discussion about empowerment-based leadership. Experienced ESFL instructors also suggested new topics to include in updating this new edition.

Developing the *Empowerment Skills for Leaders* Handbook and the accompanying Instructors Manual has been an iterative process, reflecting the thoughtful feedback of instructors, participants, and curriculum reviewers. We are grateful for their conscientious and gracious assistance.

Criteria for becoming an *Empowerment Skills for Leaders* instructor

Empowerment Skills for Leaders translates the core components and practices of empowerment-based family support presented in the *Empowerment Skills for Family Workers* curriculum within the context of relationships and mission of family-serving organizations. For this reason, *Empowerment Skills for Leaders* instructors need to have a good understanding of the *Empowerment Skills for Family Workers* concepts and the FDC credentialing process. Experienced FDC instructors with two or more years of supervisory experience are strong candidates. A master's degree in education, psychology, social work, or a related field is also required.

Prospective leadership instructors submit applications to attend an FDC Leadership Instructor's Training Institute that describe their past supervisory and group facilitation experience, and their reasons for wanting to become a leadership instructor. Upon acceptance, they attend a 2.5-day train-the-trainer institute. Leadership instructors are also required to attend a National FDC–led Update at least once every three years to remain active. Most recently, FDC Updates are presented as webinars and are offered at least once a year.

The Leadership Credential

Requirements for receiving the National Family Development Leadership Credential administered by the University of Connecticut are:

- Attendance to all sessions of the 30-hour *Empowerment Skills for Leaders* course facilitated by a certified National FDC instructor.
- Development of a Leadership Portfolio—which applies the concepts of empowerment-based leadership—by working with a "peer advisor."

Leadership Portfolio

The FDC Leadership Portfolio is a compilation of skills practices and reflections demonstrating a leader's understanding and practice of empowerment-based leadership. Portfolios are developed throughout the course. Leaders work with one another for each chapter, serving as peer advisors and providing verbal and written feedback.

Components of the Leadership Portfolio are:

- One *Independent Learning Project for each of the five chapters*. Suggestions for projects are listed at the end of each chapter, but leaders are encouraged to develop their own projects relevant to their workplace.

- One *Leadership Empowerment Plan* that identifies a short-term goal and outlines the steps to achieve it. Leaders reflect on their own strengths and challenges, applying the concepts learned in this course.

- An *Overall Reflection* at the end of the course that summarizes what they have learned, initial results of their Leadership Empowerment Plan, and how they will continue to implement the skills and concepts of empowerment-based leadership.

Completed portfolios are submitted by the instructor to National FDC for review. Upon approval, the FDC Leadership Credential is issued by the University of Connecticut.

College Credit and Contact Hours

College credit for earning the FDC Leadership Credential is available. For the most up-to-date information on number of credits and fees, contact the National FDC Program Manager at nationalfdc@uconn.edu or check the FDC website (www.familydevelopmentcredential.org) for information and application forms.

Contact hours (Continuing Education Units) are also available. Participants can receive contact hours for each hour they attend the course. Sign-in/sign-out sheets from the instructor are submitted with the application.

Application forms for both college credit and contact hours are on the FDC website.

A brief history of the Family Development Credential (FDC)

The National Family Development Credential (FDC) Program has been pioneering a paradigm shift from the "deficit" family support model to an "empowerment-based" model since the mid-1990s. In 1990, the New York State Council on Children and Families called together fifteen major state agencies to talk about a new approach built on family strengths.

The New York Department of State's Community Services Block Grant Program, directed by Evelyn Harris, took a leadership role among the state agencies. The Department of State, through its statewide Community Action Agencies, had been experimenting with shifting its paradigm to a "family development" model. They invited Cornell University's Empowering Families Project into the discussion, because of Cornell's exemplary work in training human service workers in empowerment skills. The state agencies agreed that an interagency training and credentialing program for agency workers should be developed, beginning with front-line workers, and later offering specialized training to agency supervisors and state agency staff. The New York Department of State provided initial funding and selected Cornell to develop the FDC curriculum *Empowerment Skills for Family Workers*, train and oversee FDC facilitators, and establish a permanent training and credentialing system.

In 2010, the FDC program moved to the University of Connecticut, which now provides administrative oversight and issues the FDC credentials. National FDC Director Claire Forest continued her leadership throughout the transition. Thousands of agencies and organizations nationwide have adopted a strengths-based paradigm using the Family Development Credential curriculum.

Who attends FDC training?

The FDC course *Empowerment Skills for Family Workers* is offered to front-line family workers from a wide range of government, private, and not-for-profit agencies, as well as workers from public-sector businesses, large corporations, and educational institutions. When we use the term *family workers* or *family development workers*, we are referring to "front-line" staff members from public, private, and voluntary agencies and organizations that work directly with families.

Family development staff members often work with families across the human lifespan. This includes families with young children, teen parents, retired people, people with disabilities, and many other groups. The term *family* is also used very broadly to include individuals as well as all types of family configurations.

Family development workers may include:

- Case managers
- Family advocates
- Home health aides and direct-care workers
- Intake and social welfare workers
- Community health or nutrition workers
- Early intervention staff
- Outreach workers
- Employment and training counselors
- Crisis intervention staff
- Home visitors
- Parenting educators
- Youth development/after-school program staff
- Volunteers and paid staff in faith-based groups

Other professionals, such as teachers, utility company customer advocates, probation and police officers, clergy, and supervisors of front-line family workers have also attended training and earned their Family Development Credential. Many Community Action Agencies (sometimes called Economic Opportunity Councils), Cooperative Extension Associations, and county Departments of Social Services have also trained their entire front-line staff in Family Development Credential.

How the Family Development Credential works

To earn the Family Development Credential, workers take the 90-hour *Empowerment Skills for Family Workers* course offered by FDC-certified, community-based instructors, prepare a portfolio documenting their competencies in strength-based family supports, and pass a credentialing exam. Portfolios are reviewed by National FDC Portfolio Reviewers, and exams are graded by the National FDC Program Manager. When the portfolio is approved and the worker passes the exam, the FDC credential is awarded by the University of Connecticut.

FDC instructors are trained by National FDC or affiliated states that have an approved agreement with National FDC to be state coordinators, and most often include:

- Community agency professionals with training and facilitation experience
- Faculty (regular and adjunct) in community college Human Services programs or four-year Social Work programs

- Representatives of state-level agencies interested in promoting family development within their departments or programs

Prospective instructors must have approval from their sponsoring organization and attend a 3.5-day FDC Instructors Institute. Each participant in the course is also assigned a Portfolio Advisor, who serves as a coach, mentor, and guide through the portfolio development process. Advisors are selected by FDC instructors, who provide an orientation for them before the course begins. The role of the Portfolio Advisor is integral to helping workers prepare a portfolio that demonstrates their knowledge, skills, and competencies learned throughout the training.

FDC portfolio development

FDC portfolios for *Empowerment Skills for Workers* are comprised of three components: Activities to Extend Learning, Skills Practices, and Family Development Plans, along with an Overall Reflection on their FDC Experience. Each worker/student is assigned a Portfolio Advisor, who serves as a mentor and supports them through the portfolio development process, providing feedback and guidance.

Activities to Extend Learning

In this part of portfolio development, a worker prepares written responses to three questions from the learning objectives listed in the Worker's Handbook at the end of each chapter. The Portfolio Advisor usually provides written feedback on these responses or may choose to share feedback during individual meetings over the course of training.

Skills Practices

Each chapter also requires completion of a skills practice to demonstrate a skill or competency learned. Portfolio Advisors meet with workers individually at this stage to help them develop and prepare practices that are meaningful and relevant to their work. After completing their skills practice, workers write a short reflection on the experience and submit this to their Portfolio Advisor for both verbal and written feedback.

Family Development Plans

The final component of the portfolio involves three Family Development Plans (an initial plan and two follow-up plans) prepared by the worker with an agency family or colleague who identifies a goal and takes steps to achieve it. After the three plans are completed, the worker writes a one-page reflection on the strengths they recognized in themselves and their family through the experience, the skills and competencies practiced, and ideas for using empowerment-based support in future work with families.

At the conclusion of FDC training, a one-page Overall Reflection summarizes what they learned from the course and how they plan to apply the concepts. The FDC Instructor, Portfolio Advisor, and worker/student all sign the Application to Receive the FDC Credential: Portfolio Checklist and Affirmations Form, verifying that the worker has satisfactorily completed all the requirements and is prepared to take the FDC Credentialing exam.

How FDC is different from other staff development programs

There are important differences between the Family Development Credential and other staff development programs:

- FDC calls for a new kind of relationship between families and the workers who want to help them.
- It builds on the strengths of workers, families and communities.
- It recognizes that important changes are needed in the policies and systems in which family members and workers live and work.
- It is based on an understanding of how power is used by agencies either to help families move out of dependency or to keep them dependent on government programs.
- It values diversity.
- It prepares and supports workers through a combination of classroom study and practical application, guided by a Portfolio Advisor.
- It is a competency-based training model that also facilitates learning at a deeper, experiential, self-directed, and potentially transformative level.

What the FDC research shows

The Family Development Credential Program has been evaluated over the years through several different research studies using various designs and with varied groups of program participants. Below are some of the more recent findings.

In a 2015 study by the University of Connecticut's Center for the Study of Culture, Health and Human Development, the process and effects of FDC training undertaken by a large municipality focusing on staff in its Youth Recreation division, found:[iii]

- There was an increase in workers' sense that their job allowed them to fulfill valued goals and interests. They reported feeling more creative and felt a better "fit" between their values and job opportunities.
- Staff and supervisors recognized the need for FDC, in terms of going beyond the standard trainings to address communication and problem solving. Other themes included better communication between youth and co-workers, staff having a better sense of their contribution, getting more input from the community on service needs, and more collaborative, respectful relationships among staff at different levels.
- A quote from one supervisor: "The people who have gone through the FDC trainings have actually put a better effort towards their work. … I think it's helped them feel like they are valued and that value in turn spills over to their work and to other dealings with the patrons or the public."

A 2014 University of Connecticut study researched the effects of FDC training on workplace culture, climate, and families' experiences in three large community action agencies.[iv] They found:

- There was a distinct increase in supervisors' sense of freedom to innovate in working with families and staff. Specifically, performance expectations became less rigid, and they saw less pressure on staff to conform. Leaders at different levels perceived FDC as a positive force that complemented and added to their agencies' ongoing efforts at moving toward a strength-based model. They described improvements in staff confidence and in ways staff interacted with them, with each other, and with families. They observed greater collaboration among staff, leaders and people in the community. These leaders also noted changes in their own thinking and practices related to staff and families. Those who took the Empowerment Skills for Leaders course found it especially useful, citing more democratic leadership (e.g. in meetings), better self-care and mentoring of staff.

- Workers who had completed FDC training or worked in offices where most co-workers had received training felt more effective in their work and experienced greater cooperation from co-workers. They successfully implemented ideas and skills from the course, and identified positive changes in thinking about their, and families', strengths.

A 2009 Missouri study examined change in worker's perceptions of burnout and job satisfaction before and after they participated in Family Development Credential courses held in Missouri with these findings[v]:

- Workers who took the course reported increases of self-esteem, mastery and decreases in burnout. A comparison group who hadn't taken part in FDC training experienced changes in the opposite direction in all these areas.

In 2009, the Center for the Study of Culture, Health and Human Development at the University of Connecticut studied the effects of multiple trainings for newly hired home visitors and supervisors in a statewide program.[vi] They found:

- After an extensive, year-long period of training, home visitors were asked which curricula they found most useful in their day-to-day work. The most frequently mentioned training was the Family Development Credential.

- Home visitors felt that FDC had helped them to arrive at a more strengths-based approach to families, sharpen skills for building trusting relationships, collaborate with co-workers and other agencies and take better care of themselves.

A comprehensive listing of FDC evaluation and research studies has been compiled in a document entitled "What the Research Shows," on the FDC website (www.familydevelopmentcredential.org).

[iii] C. M. Super et al., "Implementation of Family Development Credential training in selected offices at Hartford City Hall 2012-1015," Report to the City of Hartford (Center for the Study of Culture, Health & Human Development, 2015).

[iv] C. M. Super, C. Mavridis, and S. Harkness, "The Effects of Family Development Training on the Culture and Climate of CAP Service Agencies," Report to the Connecticut Children's Trust Fund (Center for the Study of Culture, Health & Human Development, 2014).

[v] D. B. Smith, "Change in Frontline Family Workers' Burnout and Job Satisfaction: Evaluating the Missouri Family Development Credential Program," *Professional Development: The International Journal of Continuing Social Work Education* 12, no. 1 (2009): 51-60.

[vi] C. M. Super et al., "Nurturing Families Network Home Visiting Program training evaluation," Report to the Connecticut Children's Trust Fund (Center for the Study of Culture, Health & Human Development, 2009).

TABLE OF CONTENTS

CHAPTER 1
FAMILY DEVELOPMENT AND THE EMPOWERED WORKPLACE

Learning objectives

- Learn the core concepts and competencies taught in *Empowerment Skills for Family Workers,* and explore how they align with empowerment-based leadership.
- Recognize the characteristics of an empowered workplace.
- Understand the paradigm shift of "power over" to a "shared power" approach to leadership.
- Increase awareness of the difference between deficit-oriented practices and the family development approach in the workplace.
- Develop and offer services and programs consistent with the philosophy and best practices of family development.
- Through participation in community-based professional development, actualize the benefits of interagency and interdepartmental collaboration in achieving outcomes-based goals.

Leading an empowered workplace

> *"I've tried all the latest management techniques to empower my staff: trainings, incentives, even reorganization, and look what's happened! They're getting results, but now they openly question my ideas, take more risks, and need more resources! What have I done?"*

Leading an empowered workplace can sometimes feel like you've opened a "Pandora's box." In Greek mythology, Pandora was a woman endowed with great intelligence, talent, and creativity, who was given a beautiful box that she was curious about, yet hesitant to open. Her story is a useful analogy to begin thinking about the profound challenge of being an effective leader.

If Pandora were the leader of a family-serving organization today, the box might contain the untold treasures of an empowered workplace: services focused on healthy self-reliance for families, a culturally diverse and competent staff, outcomes-based programs with ongoing assessment and accountability, and a workplace environment built upon mutual respect and support. However, if Pandora opens the box hoping that its treasure will, once and for all, "empower" her workplace and resolve problems and conflicts, she will be sorely disappointed. Treasures left untapped, and collected only to be admired, can become trappings. As in the case of Pandora, it's only when leaders use these "treasures" as "tools" of transformation in their organization that they can truly realize their vision of an "empowered workplace."

Now, let's revisit Pandora's organization two years in the future. During that time, staff members have been trained to work with families using empowerment-based family support and are increasingly more proficient in the skills they need to help families. The organization has ample creative and talented staff representing diverse cultures and experiences throughout the course of life. Employees (clerical support through administration) understand how their roles and efforts contribute to the mission and success of the organization. Relationships between front-line staff and supervisors are based on mutual respect, individual strengths, and goal setting to support an organization-wide model of empowerment-based support and services for families.

Cooperative relationships with community partners to bridge or fill gaps in services have been formed or strengthened. Leaders of the organization routinely consult with family workers to assess the goals of interagency collaborations. Families feel respected, listened to, and supported in setting and achieving their own goals of healthy self-reliance and interdependence. Leading the organization through this transformation is still a daily challenge in a social and political environment in which "outcomes" and "collaboration" are now comfortable processes. The most striking difference in the organization is that relationships and actions by all employees are based on the understanding that *within each person lies a bone-deep longing for freedom, self-respect, hope, and the chance to make an important contribution to one's family, one's community, and the world.*

A bone-deep longing for freedom and self-respect

This quotation from National FDC Director Claire Forest is shared early in the *Empowerment Skills for Family Workers* training. The statement expresses the cornerstone of the family development approach, upon which a new paradigm of empowering both ourselves and others is built:

> *Within each person lies a bone-deep longing for freedom, self-respect, hope, and the chance to make an important contribution to one's family, community, and the world.*

> *Without healthy outlets for this powerful, natural longing, the desire for freedom turns into lawlessness, and the need for self-respect is expressed in aggression and violence.*

> *Without avenues to make important contributions to family, community, and the world, hopelessness translates into dependency, depression, violence, substance abuse and other forms of self-abuse.*

> *No government program can help families become self-reliant, contributing members of their communities unless it is built on a recognition of the power of this bone-deep longing for freedom, self-respect, hope, and the chance to make an important contribution.*

A paradigm represents a system of thoughts, beliefs, and actions often deeply embedded—consciously or unconsciously—in our psyches. Some beliefs (such as treating your neighbor as you wish to be treated) are adopted unconsciously from our parents, faith background, or the larger culture. When circumstances require you to revise an old belief to fit a new reality, it's natural to feel frustrated and confused. Even if you initiated the change, during the time it begins to unfold you may become hesitant, and consciously (or unconsciously) try to suppress it. However, there's another approach to shifting from an outdated paradigm to a new one. By learning to stop and examine why you do what you do, and whether you choose to continue in that default mode, you can release the grip of outdated or unconscious paradigms on your thoughts, beliefs, and actions.

Empowerment Skills for Leaders focuses on two essential paradigm shifts leaders need in order to transform the practice of effective leadership:

- From leading by "power over" to "shared power"
- From leading with a focus on "providing services" to leading with a focus on "providing empowering and compassionate support."

Many agencies with FDC-credentialed staff members have enthusiastically embraced the family development empowerment paradigm. Agencies have redefined mission statements, involved families and staff in decision making, re-designated staff positions and budget line items, redesigned their space and brochures, and revised forms to reinforce a strengths-based approach. This is usually a gradual, ongoing process accomplished over months or even years. In the process, these agencies have become respected organizational leaders in their communities. Transforming an agency takes the courage and willingness to live through some uncomfortable moments.

Empowerment Skills for Leaders will help you learn a new way to guide your organization. Welcome to a curriculum that can transform your work and your life!

Basic concepts of Family Development

Many leaders take the *Empowerment Skills for Workers* course before taking the leadership course, and thus become familiar with the strengths-based concepts their staff are striving to implement. For those who haven't taken the Workers course, and as a reinforcement for those who have, we provide an overview here. *Empowerment Skills for Leaders* builds upon these concepts and facilitates getting everyone in the organization "on the same page" toward implementing empowerment-based practice at all levels. We provide a synopsis of the chapters in this section.

A sustainable route to healthy self-reliance

In the first chapter of the *Empowerment Skills for Workers* curriculum, workers learn that the deficit model or "provision of services" approach to family support has failed to help substantial numbers of families and individuals become healthy, self-reliant members of their communities, because it is based on the following set of false assumptions:

- If families can't manage on their own, there is something wrong with them.
- Families need professionals to assess what is wrong and to prescribe services.
- If families don't follow professional's advice or it doesn't work, it must be the families' fault and the appropriate action is often to withdraw services.
- Providing services is the goal of human service agencies.
- The family is providing the worker with all the information relevant to their situation, and the family will follow up on whatever service plan we create for them.

For family-serving organizations to help families using an empowerment-based model of family support called family development, workers and leaders must shift the paradigm of power in helping relationships from "power over" to "shared power" and mutual respect. Helping families take responsible control over their own futures also requires a paradigm shift in family-serving organizations from "providing services" to offering "family support." These paradigm shifts require not only that family workers and leaders learn new skills, but also that human service organizations at local, state, and federal levels approach families in entirely different ways.

In FDC training, the goal of family development is empowerment of families and the communities they live in, so families will be able to reach their goals while fully engaged in the process. *Empowerment*, in the context of family development, is defined as:

> *a dynamic process through which families reach their own goals. No one can "empower" someone else. Empowering families means helping families reclaim their ability to dream, to restore their own capacity to take good care of themselves. This also means helping communities, states and nations to create the conditions through which families can reach their own goals, which may mean changing human service systems.*

The Core Principles of Family Development

The *Core Principles of Family Development* reflect the following attitudes, beliefs, values, and actions of workers, leaders, and family serving organizations using empowerment-based support in working with families:

1. All people, and all families, have strengths.

2. The type and degree of support each family needs varies throughout the life span.

3. Most successful families are not dependent on long-term public support. Neither are they isolated. They maintain a healthy interdependence with extended family, friends, other people, spiritual organizations, cultural and community groups, schools and agencies, and the natural environment.

4. Diversity (race, ethnicity, gender, class, family form, religion, physical and mental ability, age, sexual orientation) is an important reality in our society and is valuable. Family workers need to develop competence in working effectively with people who may be different from them or come from groups that are often not respected in our society.

5. The deficit model of family assistance, in which families must demonstrate inadequacy to receive services (and professionals decide what is best for families), is counterproductive to helping families toward healthy self-reliance through a recognition of their strengths.

6. Changing from the deficit model to the family development approach requires a whole new way of thinking about social services, not simply through more new programs. Individual workers cannot make this shift without corresponding policy changes at agency, state, and federal levels.

7. Families need coordinated services in which all the agencies they work with use a similar approach. Collaboration at the local, state, and federal levels is crucial to effective family development.

8. Families and family development workers are equally important partners in the empowerment process, with each contributing important knowledge. Workers learn as much as the families from this process.

9. Families must choose their own goals and methods of achieving them. Family development workers' roles include assisting families in setting reachable goals for their own self-reliance, providing access to services needed to reach these goals, and offering encouragement.

10. Services are provided for families to reach their goals and are not in themselves a measure of success.

11. For families to move out of dependency, helping systems must shift from a "power over" to a "power with" paradigm. Human service workers have power (which they may not recognize) because they participate in the distribution of valued resources. Workers can use that power to work with families rather than exercise power over them.

The Seven Steps of Family Development

The chapter also presents the Seven Steps of Family Development to highlight the steps workers take in building empowerment-based relationships with families. The *Seven Steps of Family Development* are:

1. The family develops a partnership with a family development worker.

2. A family development worker helps the family assess its needs and strengths. This is an ongoing process.

3. The family sets its own major goals (such as providing health care for a disabled family member or getting off public assistance) and steps toward the major goal, identifying ideas for reaching them.

4. The family development worker helps the family make a written plan for pursuing these goals, with some tasks being the responsibility of family members, and some the responsibility of the worker. Accomplishments are celebrated, and the plan is continually updated.

5. The family learns and practices skills needed to become self-reliant. This is an ongoing process.

6. The family uses services as stepping stones to reach their goals.

7. The family's sense of responsibility and self-reliance is restored. The family (and each individual within the family) is strengthened through the family development process, so they are better able to handle future challenges.

The Seven Roles of Family Development Workers

The Seven Roles of Family Development Workers are the major roles that workers have in helping families achieve goals of healthy self-reliance and interdependence with their communities. The *Seven Roles of Family Development Workers* are:

1. To help families restore their sense of self-respect, self-reliance, and hope.

2. To help families reclaim their dreams of a better life.

3. To help families assess their own strengths and needs, reflect critically on how they arrived where they are, and determine what will help them move toward self-reliance.

4. To help families create their own long- and short-term goals.

5. To help families gain access to the services they need to reach these goals.

6. To encourage families to develop their own strengths as they move toward their goals, including developing and practicing needed skills.

7. To encourage communities to support families.

Worker self-empowerment

As the training progresses, there are two chapters—Presence and Mindfulness and Taking Good Care of Yourself—that focus on worker self-empowerment helping workers to identify personal strengths and nurture supportive aspects of their work and life while gaining perspective on challenges both within and outside their control. One tool that's used is the Family Circles Assessment, which helps identify current supports and stressors in their lives. Workers learn that self-empowerment involves developing or clarifying their personal vision, time management, and goal setting, as well as creating a support system, balancing work and family life, mindfulness, and creating a stress management and wellness program.

Building mutually respectful relationships with families

Building Mutually Respectful Relationships with Families helps workers develop relationships focused on a family's *needs*, rather than an agency's *services*. Effective outreach to families also requires establishing positive relationships with *key advisors* (supporters and others including families who already find the agency's services useful) and *gatekeepers* (people whose support helps the agency do its' work, and whose negative impressions hinder it).

Communicating with skill and heart

In the chapter on Communicating with Skill and Heart, family workers learn a variety of techniques, including listening and building empathy; confronting people constructively; using communication facilitators; avoiding communication blockers; paraphrasing; using "I" messages; giving factual, emotional, and solution-based feedback; and initiating steps to resolve conflict. Workers learn how to communicate with others about "hot topics," along with guidelines to help them decide whether to share their personal lives with families they work with. The chapter describes a communication trap called the "submission-aggression loop," and explains how mutually respectful communication, or assertiveness, is enhanced through skillful listening and communicating "with skill and heart." Workers learn the importance of nonverbal communication and helpful ways to work with families who have language barriers or limited literacy.

Our diverse world

Our Diverse World explores the dynamics and influences of culture on the family development process. Family workers develop awareness and understanding of how families perceive power differences, as well as how prejudice, discrimination, oppression, displacement, and immigration affect cultural awareness and cultural humility.

Assessment and goal planning

Through discussion of assessment and goal planning, workers learn why agencies still use deficit-based assessment and how to apply seven empowerment-based principles to a family's current situation and future goals. Workers learn that empowerment-based assessment involves working *with*—instead of *for*—families, collecting only the information that's needed, developing assessment tools that are culturally appropriate, and treating information with respect for confidentiality. The chapter explains the differences, advantages, and disadvantages of standardized and individualized assessments.

Home visiting

Learning ways to use a family development approach during Home Visiting prepares workers for entering a family's home for the first time, and to manage unannounced visits. Workers learn helpful ways to maintain contact with families between visits, as well as how to stay focused during interruptions. This chapter also covers safety measures that are important for a variety of different home visiting situations.

Helping families access specialized services

In Helping Families Access Specialized Services, workers learn how to help families recognize the need for specialized services in areas such as developmental disabilities, common mental health problems, domestic violence (including child abuse), and alcohol and drug dependency among others. They learn the importance of helping with follow-through on referrals and providing appropriate support for families who use them.

Collaboration and community support

Collaboration and Community Support helps workers understand why systems-level interventions are sometimes needed to help families become self-reliant. Workers learn to assess the reasons for collaboration through discussion of the *Keys to Successful Collaboration* and the *Practical Pitfalls* (and how to turn them into advantages). This chapter also teaches workers how to help families advocate for themselves, offering guidelines for communicating with elected officials and other community leaders.

Family Development Credential Training is a competency-based training program with flexibility to support workers in reaching goals related to personal development as well as building professional competencies. In the next section, you'll learn about **how** workers learn through FDC training to better understand the impact of empowerment-based training on staff as individuals and co-workers.

The learning process

Workers learn skills to assist families in achieving goals of healthy self-reliance in various ways: personal experience, higher education, professional training, first-hand experience working with families, or a combination of any of these.

Adults learn in qualitatively different ways than school children. More often, adults use a combination of knowledge, observation, and experience, rather than instructional techniques like rote memorization and practice. Adults decide "what" to learn in accordance with "how" they plan to use it.

The task of hiring a new staff member is a good example of the range of competencies you would most likely use in adult learning. To begin the process, you learn new information about the pool of applicants by reviewing their resume or application. Next, you consider each applicant based on your knowledge of the position and their stated qualifications and experience. At this time, you might draw upon your experience or intuition to assess the skills and abilities of each applicant. Then, you would interview the strongest candidates to gain first-hand knowledge about their individual strengths. You might develop a list of questions to discuss with each candidate to compare the range of responses. During the interview, you would observe their body language. After the interviews, you reflect on how each person's qualifications and personality will potentially build upon, or complement, the position and your entire organization. You do some critical thinking to analyze factors that distinguish candidates from each other. Finally, you make your selection for the position using the sum of your knowledge, intuition, and experience you've gained throughout the process, and you incorporate the philosophy and values of the organization in your decision.

When delegating assignments and beginning new projects, you need to continuously assess knowledge and skills of staff members. If you're like most leaders, at times you may have assessed a worker's level of knowledge and skill as less than it was and been pleasantly surprised with the results. Sometimes, you may have assessed their level of knowledge and skill as being more than it was and been confused or disappointed with the outcome.

Simply looking at educational background, professional training, personality, or past experiences isn't enough for most leaders to have full confidence in what a staff member knows. You've invested (or are considering investing) considerable time and resources in training for front-line workers. Leading an empowered workplace depends on being able to trust your assessment of their skills and competencies. You've read about the knowledge and types of skills that workers learn in FDC training. But you also need to find out *how* they learn to direct their knowledge and skills toward providing the best possible service to families and to your agency.

This leads to the question: How do workers learn to apply knowledge and skills in becoming effective family workers?

Instrumental learning

For most adults, skills develop into competencies through the first level of learning, called *instrumental*—or "how to"—learning. In FDC training, a wide variety of instructional techniques are used to facilitate instrumental learning: case studies, simulations, role plays, brainstorming, visualization, self-assessment, paired and small group activities, large group discussions, panel presentations, lecturettes, and worksheets. Most people have preferences for how they learn (e.g., "I'm a visual learner"), and some can even identify the types of activities that best stimulate their learning.

Instrumental learning is the most basic level of learning, because it requires consistent reinforcement; otherwise, over time, it discontinues or reverts to its previous level. For example, in Chapter 2, Communicating with Skill and Heart, workers spend considerable time practicing techniques such as using communication facilitators and avoiding communication blockers, paraphrasing different types of feedback, and "I" messages. Workers learn "how to" develop or enhance their communication skills through sequential activities. During the session, workers give and receive feedback, usually in pairs, to support one another in shaping and refining their responses. However, even after workers complete their training, if these skills aren't continually reinforced in their current work environment, the skills begin to diminish, and eventually disappear. FDC training is more than just "how to" learning. FDC instructors facilitate the curriculum as an *interactive group process*, and portfolio development provides yet another opportunity to practice new skills outside of class. Many supervisors and leaders have reported that reading the *Empowerment Skills for Family Workers: A Worker Handbook* curriculum has given them a deeper understanding of what workers have learned in FDC training, and how to reinforce that learning as their skills and competencies develop.

Workers come to any learning experience with varying levels of awareness, insight, knowledge, and experience. Some workers begin FDC training with trepidation at the prospect of "going back to school," especially if their past experience with high school or college was negative. Other workers feel that further education, for them, is unnecessary. Some are excited and eager to attend.

From the first session, participants learn that FDC training is an interactive, participatory, and group-centered learning experience. Even though FDC instructors follow a curriculum outlining specific activities to stimulate discussion, each FDC session is unique. Knowledge and experience of every participant is valued and contributes to the overall success of the training

Experiential learning

A second type of adult learning is *experiential*—or "try to"—learning. FDC training allows workers to practice skills in a safe and supportive educational setting. FDC training promotes experiential learning in two ways: class-based activities conducted by an FDC instructor, and portfolio development under the guidance of a portfolio advisor. The concept of "bifocal or peripheral vision" is presented as the ability to look closely at a family's strengths, while acknowledging and assisting with their broader struggles. When planning a portfolio Skills Practice, a worker might plan to develop a relationship with a family using "bifocal vision"—identifying and sharing their strengths in an upcoming home visit. Gaining first-hand knowledge about how a concept translates into action from personal experience is an important way to understand the lifelong process of learning.

It can be disorienting when new knowledge doesn't fit an old paradigm or contradicts our current experience. Family workers quickly learn that helping families avert crises doesn't necessarily prevent future problems, or that simply helping families gain access to services doesn't prevent recurring difficulties. They understand that successful family support programs require a balance of financial, physical, and human resources. When experiential learning reveals clear discrepancies between what is "real" versus what is "ideal," the process of reflecting—or stepping back to consider our interpretation or understanding—is a valuable process of learning.

Self-directed learning

Have you ever …

- studied your family genealogy?
- taken a cooking or dance class offered in your community?
- read a book or taken a lesson to improve your golf swing?
- faced a difficult situation (e.g., illness, loss of a loved one, a parenting or job change) and decided to learn more about how to cope?

These activities are examples of *self-directed*—or "choose to"—learning. The characteristic of self-directed learning that distinguishes it from other types of adult learning is the freedom and independence for you to learn at your own level and pace.

Facilitating self-directed learning is quite different than the more traditional role of a typical teacher in adult education settings. Instead of a curriculum-centered relationship in which a teacher is perceived as an "expert" or "authority," a facilitator's primary role in self-directed learning is to help learners develop their own abilities to direct their own learning, and to encourage personal growth and development through the process. Self-directed learning usually involves high levels of motivation and responsibility, sequential learning activities, and reflecting on personal experience. This process is often very personal; the end result often contributes to improved health and well-being. For that reason, it's unlikely that those who adopt the conventional role of teacher and trainer can ever "teach" self-directed learning. Teachers, trainers, and facilitators who encourage and support self-direction develop unique and mutually enriching relationships with learners, and as a result, often observe tremendous strides in a learner's personal and professional development.

In FDC training, workers choose ways to develop their skills through the process of portfolio development. In Activities to Extend Learning, workers choose three questions that range from factual responses such as "List three ways of establishing a respectful relationship on a first home visit" to sharing life experiences such as "Give an example from your life of the following kinds of assessments: professional judgment, standardized assessment, tests."

Some questions at the end of each chapter provide encouragement for self-directed learning through questions such as:

- Where does your own self-respect come from? What diminishes it?
- Ask your own family members questions about relatives, places, immigration, celebrations, losses, and role models. Record or write down what they tell you. Ask them to review what you've written or recorded, adding anything they suggest that makes the history more accurate.

Another avenue of self-directed learning involves completing three Family Development Plans over the course of FDC training. This component helps a worker gain practical experience in helping a family (an actual agency family, or "volunteer" family) to prepare and assess a plan outlining a major goal that involves both the worker and family member(s) in its accomplishment. Workers practice ways to help families identify their own goals and the steps to achieve them. The worker and family identify and prepare an initial Family Development Plan (including a goal, steps that the worker and family will take to achieve it, the family's strengths and concerns, and resource information) and two follow-up plans.

As workers help families create Family Development Plans, they gain insight into the self-directed learning process for families: creating steps to achieve personal goals, helping families learn skills, and encouraging personal growth. Outcomes that reflect a worker's increased capacity for self-directed learning might include developing career and educational goals, starting health and wellness programs, and increasing knowledge and understanding of other cultures.

Transformative learning[1]

Sometimes, adult learning results in profound changes in a person's perception and interpretation of life experience. This type of learning is called *transformative*—or "to make meaning of"—learning. Unexpected life events (e.g., the sudden death of a loved one) or circumstances occurring over a period of years (e.g., leaving an abusive relationship) could prompt a person to revise or change their most deeply held beliefs and values. Fortunately, a person's search for the purpose and meaning of life doesn't have to be undertaken in the wake of a catastrophe or crisis. At any time in life—and frequently during major transitions (e.g., when grown children leave home, at retirement)—transformative learning begins as a period of feeling disoriented and uncomfortable with a new life role.

The process of transformation through adult learning is complex and often involves these experiences: feeling confused and disoriented because deep-seated beliefs and values no longer work, cycles of questioning and reflecting, and trying out new ways to cope. Having the opportunity to discuss experiences and get feedback is central to the process of transformative learning. In experiencing personal transformation, a person often learns about the types of "filters" (e.g., gender, race, ethnicity, sexual orientation) she/he has been using to relate to life experience. With a deeper understanding for the types of filters that limit ability to see life experience clearly, a person can expand their knowledge and understanding in more inclusive ways. Workers who begin to experience steps in a transformative learning during FDC training find that class sessions and portfolio development can be a deeply enlightening and liberating experience. Transforming old belief and value systems into more inclusive and expansive ones through training activities and reflection helps workers connect the learning experience with their ongoing journey of personal growth and development.

 In FDC training, activities, and discussion, help workers increase their critical reflection skills (a process of transformative learning) by contrasting the deficit approach with a new conceptual model called "family development." Workers are asked to reflect on the need for the paradigm shift from a "deficit" ("power over") approach to a "family development" ("power with"/"shared power") approach in family support.

Workers learn the underpinnings of the family development process through the:

- Core principles underlying an empowerment and family support approach to family development
- Seven steps of family development
- Seven roles of family development workers

For most workers, the mismatch between the deficit model and values inherent in human service work becomes apparent early in the training, and typically results in either of two types of opposing responses:

- "This approach to working with families is the one that I've been waiting and hoping for!"
- "This approach will never work!"

As workers question and reflect on their viewpoints, FDC training creates the physical and emotional space in which to discuss their perceptions and reshape their beliefs in a supportive and organized way. Workers report that FDC training and portfolio development is often a safe haven in which to examine the origins of their belief systems and values. The following is a Skills Practice Reflection excerpt from a worker whose participation in FDC gave her the courage to attend an Alanon meeting:

> *Understanding who I am as a result of my past experiences has been just the tip of the iceberg for me. I told another person at the meeting that for so long I denied and hid the fact that I was a child of an alcoholic—but I'm realizing that the qualities I have in light of that experience are some of my best strengths. Doing this skills practice helped me connect to a place that used to be so painful, but with the support I received doing the thing I feared most, it's become a place and source of strength.*

For many workers, FDC training acts as a "springboard" from which to view life experience on a different level. Those who enroll in FDC training with trepidation based on negative past experiences of higher education find that it validates their experience and knowledge—that all people and families have strengths that need and deserve support. For entry-level or mid-career family development professionals, FDC training is an excellent refresher course for enhancing professional skills and abilities to build healthy, empowering relationships. For those with college education or specialized training, FDC is a unique professional development opportunity to update skills, network with other service providers in a noncompetitive setting, and expand their knowledge of community-based resources. And for those who are skeptical and think that no wave of reform can ever change a "perfectly imperfect" family support system, FDC training helps them voice their frustrations, and invites them to envision and enact ways to create a more equitable system.

To really know what a worker learns through FDC training, we recommend that you speak with staff members or colleagues who are taking or have taken the course and earned their credential. If the agency has implemented FDC training for workers across different programs or departments, speak with workers who represent the variety of empowerment-based services and support across your agency. Here are our suggestions for how to do this:

- Encourage people to share their knowledge and understanding openly. Explain why you're interested in knowing more about FDC training. You'll ultimately want to know how FDC training is affecting the agency's "bottom line" in productivity and measurable outcomes. But right now, learning how FDC training is affecting your staff **is** the outcome. This step is analogous to the way workers need to approach families in building a trusting and respectful relationship. You can collect rich, qualitative information about how workers and staff develop critical relationships with families right now.

- Ask them about the concepts and skills they're learning, the types of training activities they find helpful, and how the training has affected their relationships with families and colleagues.

Characteristics of an empowered workplace

In *Empowerment Skills for Family Workers*, participants learn that to help families develop self-respect and practice skills of healthy self-reliance, they must first build a partnership with families based on shared power. The same holds true for the relationship between a worker and supervisor. Supervisors and leaders are the organizational role models for workers and staff in learning how to think, reflect, and act in making the paradigm shift from "power over" to "shared power."

An agency leader at a focus group summarized the sentiments of many supervisors and leaders:

> *One of the biggest plusses about the FDC program is the common knowledge and language it promotes within and across agencies. But supervisors need to get the same curriculum and learn the same language as front-line workers. Because you can't have one group doing it and the other group not.*

In other words, everyone in the agency should be "on the same page" to effectively implement the principles of family development and empowerment-based leadership.

The dictionary definition of "empower" is "to give authority to," yet the word can have different meanings to different people, depending on their unique experiences and perspectives. Here are some characteristics of an empowered workplace for you to consider:

- Creative and talented employees who represent diverse cultures and experiences across the life course.
- Employees who understand their role and how their individual efforts contribute to the agency and its overall mission.
- Employees and supervisors who are committed to creating relationships based on mutual respect, recognizing individual strengths, and working on common goals.
- Employees who feel respected, listened to, and welcomed.
- Leaders who build and strengthen cooperative relationships within the agency and the community to share resources and address gaps in services.
- Leaders who understand that each person has a bone-deep longing for freedom, safety, self-respect, hope, and the chance to make important contributions to one's family, to one's community, and to the world.

Are you skeptical about whether you can lead effectively if you don't use the "power over" approach? Are you a bit concerned about how you can carry out your responsibilities unless you retain your power? Good—read on! Changing from the "power over" mode to "shared power" does *not* mean you become powerless and ineffective. Instead, it suggests new ways to work skillfully with the powerful, inevitable societal changes of a paradigm shift to empowerment-based family support. These changes are discouraging leaders who cling to the old paradigm, while energizing leaders skillful in using a shared power approach.

The "power over" approach of family assistance is based on these faulty assumptions:

- Families who need support must have something wrong with them.
- Professionals know what's best for families.
- Using incentives and sanctions builds healthy self-reliance.
- Providing services is the goal of human service agencies.

An agency manager or supervisor using a "power over" approach might make similar assumptions about workers:

- The supervisor knows all the relevant information about situations that involve staff members.
- Supervisors and leaders know what's best for staff.
- Unless monitored closely, staff members will be lazy and dishonest
- Staff members will follow up on whatever is recommended.

Supervisors and leaders who use a "shared power" approach assume that workers:

- Know their strengths and challenges best
- Are most successful in accomplishing plans they create in consultation with their supervisor, not plans supervisors make for them
- See their role with staff members as assisting them in recognizing their strengths and challenges
- Support staff members in accomplishing mutually agreed upon goals

The deficit model teaches us to see the helping relationship as one in which those seeking help bring nothing to the table, while professionals bring their training, experience, and knowledge of available resources. The "power with" model recognizes that each partner brings valuable information and abilities to the table. Workers often know their own jobs best, have goals and dreams about how to reach them, and often have many of the practical skills needed to do so. Adapting information presented in Empowerment Skills for Family Workers, the following table highlights the differences between a worker's and supervisor's response to an empowerment ("power with") or deficit ("power over") approach.

Concept	Shared Power	"Power Over" Approach
Worker's frame of reference	"I am responsible for my goals and future."	"The organization owes it to me"
Worker-supervisor relationship	Mutual respect for one another's talents and roles. Worker and Supervisor develop and set goals together.	Supervisor decides what a worker needs Supervisor assumes a worker is not competent so must be constantly monitored
Supervisor's frame of reference	What is strong with this worker (and how can I help them build on it)?	What is wrong with this worker (and how can I make them fix it)?
Supervisor's focus	Focus on supporting ongoing professional development.	Focus on current crisis.
Power dynamic	Power "with"	Power "over"
Supervisor's view of diversity	Individual differences and staff diversity are valuable.	Workers should "fit in"

The empowerment approach/deficit approach

An understanding of power is important for both supervisors and workers, because power—and its use or abuse—influences whether workers stay dependent or become self-reliant, and whether they are effective or ineffective. Simply put, understanding power in worker-supervisor relationships also helps supervisors support workers in building mutually respectful and effective partnerships with families.

Power is an uncomfortable concept for many people. Almost everyone has had a bad experience with abusive power that resulted in feelings of anger or betrayal. When most people talk about power, they refer to a person or institution having power over others.

Family members are well aware of the dynamics of power. They know that family workers have power over resources that they need, such as money, housing, food, education, and jobs. When family members and family workers share power, there's agreement on the purpose of the partnership and recognition of what each partner brings. In a "shared power" relationship, workers help family members to clarify their goals, and to create and follow a practical plan for reaching them. Essentially, the relationship teaches family members the skills to manage future problems themselves—the skills of healthy self-reliance.

If a family worker has the need for power over the family, it's hard to build a shared-power relationship. A family worker may have ideas about helping that the family member doesn't find helpful. A worker may become disappointed in the family member not moving forward quickly in accordance with the worker's ideas.

Parallel situations often exist in the workplace. Supervisors have power over resources workers need, such as raises, computers, agency cars, office space, and secretarial support. For example, a family worker may ask their supervisor about continuing to work with a family on goals after funding or services have officially concluded. In a "power over" relationship, the supervisor's decision might be motivated by the attitude that funding or time limits regulate relationships between workers and families. In this situation, the supervisor plays the role of an "enforcer" rather than a "facilitator" in supporting goals of the worker-family relationship. A "power over" structure in a supervisor-worker relationship can hinder a worker's ability to develop mutually respectful relationships with families in two ways:

1. The worker may choose to model their relationship with the family in accordance with the supervisor-worker relationship.

2. The worker may not be willing to risk a confrontation with their supervisor to continue to support the family's needs.

A supervisor–staff member relationship built on "shared power" can help staff develop the ability to manage routine problems with little intervention from the supervisor. In a "shared power" relationship, the supervisor's decision is motivated by the desire to balance funding and time limits with the goals and outcomes of a family development relationship. In this situation, the supervisor trusts that a worker's extension request for a family merits consideration, and the supervisor and worker discuss the variety of options available. The final decision about whether to continue with a family, to provide referral and transitional support, or to conclude services is made by trusting the worker's perception of the situation. In the end, even if the worker and supervisor don't agree on the final decision, mutual respect and trust is demonstrated, and ultimately the relationship is strengthened.

Although it might appear to be at first, the "power over" approach is neither cost-effective nor efficient. In the long run, it costs more for the helping organization to continue dealing with a family's problem than it does to work in-depth to help them set and reach goals they believe in, and to help them become more self-reliant in solving their problems with less agency intervention in the future. Moreover, it takes additional time and money for a supervisor to be consulted continually on routine matters.

The effect of this paradigm shift on your organization and community

The deficit model originated in the welfare programs of the last century, in which churches and other organizations provided food, shelter, and other basic services to society's unfortunates. The current human service structure has also been influenced by the medical system, in which expert doctors diagnose people's problems and prescribe treatment. In these systems, families are forced to demonstrate what's wrong before they can get the services they need. In the empowerment approach, we assume that family members know best what their strengths and problems are, and that they will be successful in solving problems through setting and accomplishing goals they've created.

As family-serving agencies shift from the deficit model and "provision of service" paradigm to an empowerment-based family development approach, a temporary period of disequilibrium often occurs. Just as the natural environment is affected by the ways in which human beings use air, water, and land, communities are affected by the way organizations provide family assistance, including:

- Legislation that provides large amounts of funding for programs targeted for specific groups
- Changes in political or funding support for established programs
- Stricter eligibility requirements
- Creation or elimination of agencies
- Competition among organizations for the same funding
- Funding increasingly being based on outcomes, rather than on services provided
- Local incidents that draw attention to problems, making an organization and its work highly visible—positively or negatively.

We live in a time when the impact of technology and social change is having an enormous effect on families and the entire family support system. In *Social Work at the Millennium: Critical Reflections on the Future of the Profession*,[2] June Gary Hopps and Robert Morris describe seven powerful social forces affecting communities in the new millennium that are just as relevant today as they were at the turn of the century. We paraphrase them here:

- The paradox between economic prosperity and inequality (the widening gap between the "haves" and "have nots")
- The changing structure, role, and function of families
- The cultural impact of new waves of immigration and resettlement
- Violence in families, the workplace, and communities
- The challenge of racial and gender diversity and leadership
- People living longer
- Recognizing spirituality as an essential component in healing

To this list, we add these other factors:
- Economic globalization
- Increasing recognition of worldwide environmental interdependence and climate change
- Technology and social media
- Vanishing privacy
- The opioid epidemic
- Political divisiveness

Making the paradigm shift from a deficit approach to an empowerment approach will have impact at every level of the family service system. If we think about the ongoing process of empowerment in a broad-based family support system that builds upon itself, it might look like this:

Effects of the paradigm shift from deficit to empowerment at the family service system level

START HERE and read clockwise
Leaders of family-serving agencies support worker and allocate adequate resources for family-focused programs and services.

Workers in family-serving agencies help families reclaim their ability to dream and to create, plan, and achieve goals of healthy self-reliance.

Families become increasingly more self-reliant, contributing members of their communities.

National and local family support associations raise awareness about family support practice and strengthen local advocacy efforts.

Family-serving agencies work cooperatively and collaboratively in their communities to achieve family-focused outcomes and bridge gaps in services.

The individual experiences her/his bone-deep longing for freedom, self-respect, hope, and the chance to make an important contribution to her/his family, community, and the world.

National and state elected officials enact legislation that promotes family-centered support to families across the lifespan.

Funding sources support programs that demonstrate how innovative programs and inter-agency collaboration help famlies achieve healthy interdependence with their communities.

Policymakers develop procedures and guidelines that demonstrate and strengthen the committment to involve families in the process of family development.

Whenever one member of the broad-based family support system acts in a way that recognizes the need for balance and interrelationship between all members, another advance in the paradigm shift from deficit to empowerment occurs. For example, when funders support innovative collaborations of family-serving agencies, and as family-serving associations provide opportunities for family members to actively participate in shaping family support policies with community leaders and elected officials, enormous advances can occur.

Creating a "Gracious Space"

Empowerment-based leadership is not only about the approach that you use, it is also about creating an environment that is conducive to learning and engagement. The Center for Ethical Leadership has developed a core body of work called "Gracious Space,"[3] which is defined as *"a spirit and setting where we invite the stranger and learn in public."* It's essentially a process that values inclusion and diversity by creating an environment that welcomes diverse opinions, intentionally listens, and promotes learning together.

It's likely that you've experienced Gracious Space without this name attached to it. The four elements—spirit, setting, invite the stranger, and learn in public—may seem simple to understand, but they aren't necessarily easy to put into practice. Here's a brief description of the four elements:

- *Spirit* is about creating a supportive environment. This can be accomplished in many ways, such as conveying a welcoming attitude, having compassion for someone experiencing a difficult situation, taking the time to get to know a new staff member, or skillfully using humor during a stressful time.

- *Setting* is the actual physical environment of the workplace that supports our ability to feel productive, healthy, and connected in our work and with others. Again, there are many dimensions to this. It can include sharing food, a comfortable temperature in the office, expressing your personality through art, or facilitating opportunities for staff to engage with each other in meaningful ways, among others.

- *Invite the stranger* borrows a term from Parker Palmer, who defined "stranger" as any individual who is not typically involved in the conversation or process. This could be someone from a different background, perspective, ethnicity, gender, position within the agency, or who possesses any other quality that makes them seem different. Inviting the stranger to participate in the decision-making process broadens our viewpoints and creates new opportunities.

- *Learn in public* applies the intentional listening and learning you've previously gathered. It requires a willingness to explore assumptions and let go of the "right way" of doing things. It means opening your heart and being willing to change your mind.

In Gracious Space, people listen more and judge less. In this space, we can work better across boundaries, share diverse perspectives, work through conflict, discover transformative solutions, and carry out innovations for change. In future chapters, we'll explore some strategies for creating Gracious Space.

Pioneers in changing the "power over" paradigm

Helping organizations in areas such as health care and children's services, as well as higher education and large corporations, have begun to shift from the "professionals know best" approach to one that values families' and workers' strengths. For example, in the New Zealand model of child and youth welfare, legislation requires that professionals offer families a major voice in keeping children safe and healthy and within the extended family system whenever possible.

In the 1970s, the Cornell Family Matters Project applied the first longitudinal study of family strengths to 276 families in Syracuse, NY. This landmark study, headed by Dr. Moncrieff Cochran, coined the term "parental empowerment," and went on to train home visitors in the skills needed to work with families' strengths.

In the 1990s, the New York State Council on Children and Families brought together fifteen major family-service state agencies to determine how to move their modes of practice toward this new strengths-based approach. Of these, the Department of State's Community Services Block Grant Program, directed by Evelyn Harris, took a lead role in providing funding to develop an interagency training and credentialing program for frontline family workers, which became the National Family Development Credential Program (FDC). Having started in New York State, the FDC Program has now expanded to many states across the country.

More recently, Molloy College, in Long Island, NY, offered *Empowerment Skills for Leaders* to its department heads and other college leaders, and has enjoyed tremendous success. They have recognized that family development concepts taught in FDC are just as relevant in working with their students—and with each other—to develop stronger collaborative efforts throughout the college and in the broader community.

In the realm of health care, major health insurance plans now pay for services that teach people to take a major role in their own health care, such as diabetes management classes and "smoking cessation" workshops. Worldwide, the most effective business leaders meet regularly with employees, and then try out the ideas they come up with together.

Empowering leadership: Pitfalls and potential

Leading an empowered workplace can be both exhilarating and frustrating. As employees in your organization begin to recognize that a deficit-based approach has only sustained dependency and the inability of families to move toward healthy self-reliance as well as their own professional development, they will reflect on and choose to make the paradigm shift to "empowerment" in their professional and personal relationships. As they practice and develop competencies in supporting families and co-workers, it's natural that they will also want to develop an empowerment-based relationship *with you*.

Initially, this shift could create challenges for you as a leader or supervisor. You'll need patience and perseverance to overcome the inevitable pitfalls you'll encounter as your organization goes through the process of transformation. And to be sure, once you've taken the initial steps through staff training and development to create an empowering workplace for workers and families, there will be times when you feel as if you've opened a Pandora's box.

Staff members who are self-empowered strive to build mutually respectful relationships with families, co-workers, and their supervisors. They communicate openly, genuinely, and honestly, and recognize strengths and state their needs in positive and assertive ways. They want to make an important contribution and are willing to ask for the resources to achieve those results. The most significant pitfalls that interfere with the process of empowering leadership tend to occur when leaders:

- Bounce back and forth between "power over" and "power with" approaches with staff members and collaborators
- Cling to the outdated "deficit"-based paradigm of providing services, which requires workers to use incentives and sanctions to develop a family's healthy self-reliance
- Fail to acknowledge social forces and organizations at the local, state, and national levels that are already transforming the way agencies are helping families

At the beginning of this chapter, we described how opening Pandora's box, as a metaphor for your own vision of an empowered workplace, can reveal these treasures:

- Services focused on healthy self-reliance for those you serve
- A culturally diverse and competent staff who are motivated to do their best
- Outcome-based programs with ongoing assessment and accountability
- A workplace environment built upon mutual respect and cooperation

Now, we'll add one more element of invaluable significance to that list: making your own important contribution to family, organization, community, and the world through leadership that values the bone-deep longing for freedom, self-respect, and hope in the people you lead and in yourself. The transforming potential of empowering leadership is much more than the far-reaching contributions you'll provide to your organization and community. It's the opportunity and challenge to claim for yourself the same potential you are developing and nurturing in others.

---

[1] Transformative learning theory was developed by Jack Mezirow at Teachers College, Columbia University.

[2] J. Gary Hopps and R. Morris, eds., Social Work at the Millennium: Critical Reflections on the Future of the Profession. (New York: Free Press, 2000).

[3] Patricia M. Hughes, *Gracious Space: A Practical Guide for Working Together Better* (Seattle, WA: Center for Ethical Leadership, 2004).

Chapter 1—Additional Resources

Books

Bolea, Al, and Leanne Atwater. Applied Leadership Development: Nine Elements of Leadership Mastery. London: Routledge, 2015.

Cranton, Patricia. Professional Development as Transformative Learning: New Perspectives for Teachers and Adults. San Francisco: Jossey-Bass, 1996.

Howell, Jon P., and Isaac Wanasika. *Snapshots of Great Leadership.* London: Routledge, 2018.

Forest, Claire. *Empowerment Skills for Family Workers.* Ithaca, NY: Forest Home Press, 2015.

Merriam, Sharan B., and Rosemary S. Caffarella. *Learning in Adulthood: A Comprehensive Guide.* San Francisco: Jossey-Bass, 1999.

Mezirow, Jack, and Associates. Learning as Transformation: Critical Perspectives on a Theory in Progress. San Francisco: Jossey-Bass, 2004.

Articles

Bednarz, T. F. "Seven Key Benefits of an Empowered Workplace." Blogpost, 2012. https://majorium.wordpress.com/2012/02/09/seven-key-benefits-of-an-empowered-workplace/.

Bednarz, T. F. "Defining the Empowered Leader." Blogpost, 2013. https://majorium.wordpress.com/2012/10/30/defining-the-empowered-leader/.

Ruder, K. "Gracious Space: Holding the Dynamics of Collective Leadership and Community Change." Kaleel Jamison Consulting Group, 2009. http://www.ethicalleadership.org/uploads/2/6/2/6/26265761/gracious_space_holding_the_dynamics_of_collective_leadership_and_community_change.pdf.

Worksheets

"Gracious Space Self-Assessment." Center for Ethical Leadership, 1401 E. Jefferson, Ste. 505, Seattle, WA 98122 (206-328-3020). www.ethicalleadership.org.

Ideas for Independent Learning Projects

The following ideas are suggestions for independent learning projects that will increase your understanding of how the family development approach can benefit your agency. A copy of the Independent Learning Project Plan form is in the Appendix. *To create a meaningful and manageable plan, you're encouraged to develop your own independent learning project relevant to your workplace, or make modifications to ones listed below.*

- Review the background information about *Empowerment Skills for Workers* in the Introduction and in Chapter 1. Develop a list of interview questions and meet with an FDC-credentialed worker to learn more about how Family Development Training has affected their work with families. Prepare a written summary about what you learned during the interview detailing ways you can support workers using FDC principles and practices in your workplace.

- Think about how you and your agency might become more involved or supportive in promoting the family development approach with community partners. Write a "draft" memo to staff sharing your ideas about the experience and suggest ways you and your staff can work together to integrate a family development approach across agency programs.

Chapter 2
Transforming Your Workplace through Empowerment-Based Leadership

Learning objectives

- Learn how the family development approach aligns with models of effective leadership.
- Reflect on your personal leadership style and how it may vary with different staff members.
- Recognize the natural assets of staff members and strengths of the organization.
- Align your leadership vision with the mission of your organization.
- Assess the level of empowerment in your workplace.
- Understand the different types of organizational change and ways to build your agency's capacity for transformation.
- Identify key components of family-focused and outcome-based program assessment and compare them to what your agency is currently using.
- Strengthen interagency collaborations.
- Learn about and connect with state and national family support initiatives.

Are *you* ready?

Before leaving on a business trip or vacation, you probably look through your suitcase a few times to make sure you've got everything you need. You might prepare a "to do" checklist or write a list of information others need to know so things run smoothly while you're away. Travel that takes you far away from home involves planning and thoughtful preparation. You might read tour books, look up information on the Internet, and talk with people who have visited your destination. You may try to imagine the sights, sounds, and tastes of a different culture. As a traveler and visitor, you need to be open-minded and plan for the unexpected.

When you return after such a trip to a different location and culture, sometimes you feel changed as a result of that experience. Perhaps you're more aware of similarities you share with that culture and more appreciative of your differences. Sometimes, even a simple change in physical location can help you to see the "bigger picture" and gain a clearer perspective on the world, and on your situation at home.

As you think about transforming your workplace through empowerment-based leadership, the analogy of preparing for a trip is a useful one. If you're planning a simple trip across town, you prepare by thinking about how to get there, and the time and cost involved. Taking a trip out of town requires more preparation. You may need to coordinate your travel with schedules of public transportation and plan for some downtime between connections. Likewise, the journey of transforming your workplace through empowerment-based leadership will teach you important and timeless insights. It will require time, preparation, reflection, and practice. Are you ready? If so, read on!

Leadership

It's not easy being a leader! You probably deal with unhappy and unproductive workers, programs that are underfunded and/or are making discouragingly slow progress, and regulations and procedures that are cumbersome and tedious. In addition, you may have personal financial worries because your salary doesn't adequately reward you for the difficult work you do. Yet with all these challenges, you strive to lead your agency's work while protecting its financial stability and enhancing its reputation in the community.

What's your ideal of true leadership? This question might bring to mind visionaries such as Dr. Martin Luther King, Jr., Mahatma Gandhi, Eleanor Roosevelt, or Nelson Mandela. As you reflect on such ideal leaders and their characteristics, talents, and abilities, it's natural to focus on their extraordinary accomplishments. Yet true leaders have a special quality that transcends the magnitude of their accomplishments: *the ability to be aware, awake, mindful, and fully present in their lives.* This chapter will help you become even more effective in your leadership role as you transform your organization using empowerment-based leadership while developing the ability to empower yourself and live a more balanced life.

Making two paradigm shifts

There are two paradigm shifts necessary for developing, implementing, and maintaining empowerment-based leadership skills in your life and work:

- The shift from "power over" to "shared power"
- The shift from leadership that focuses on "providing services" to "providing empowering and compassionate support"

Taking a trip by hiking or sailing requires that you have a compass to help guide you safely on your way. A compass doesn't give you explicit directions for the shortest or quickest route to your destination; rather, it serves to help you determine that you're headed in the right direction. Making the paradigm shift to "shared power" and empowering, compassionate support is a journey for you and your organization. Empowerment-based leadership, like learning to travel using a compass, is the process that helps you and your organization navigate the journey of organizational transformation.

Making the paradigm shift to "shared power" doesn't mean that you simply let the people you supervise make all the decisions or do whatever they want. You continue to be responsible for the well-being of the organization and you share appropriate aspects of this responsibility. "Shared power" leadership is built on sharing responsibility and vision *with* the people you supervise. You share your own insights and expertise while listening to, and honoring, the wisdom and expertise of those you work with. It's a partnership. For example, a family worker may come to you with the agency's intake form to talk about revising the form with more strengths-based wording. Working with a staff member in a shared-power mode involves drawing on their wisdom and expertise to address the suggestion, as well as sharing your own knowledge and perspective.

Reorienting an agency and yourself from "power over" to "shared power" is a process that often takes years. You can expect troublesome—sometimes humorous—glitches along the way. In Chapter 3, Leadership and Self-Empowerment, you'll learn to listen well to your own inner wisdom, while in Chapter 4, Supervising with Skill and Heart, you'll learn to listen deeply to the people around you, even during times of conflict. Both abilities are essential to empowered leadership in today's complex human-service world.

It takes courage and confidence to work with people in a shared power relationship. Supervisors let go of their protective sense of superiority and reveal their own vulnerability, admitting that they don't always have all the answers. They do this by sharing appropriate aspects of their own lives ("I have a young child myself" or "When my own mother was in and out of hospitals, I discovered a lot about myself"), or by letting workers know they are also frustrated with the "system." The supervisor's reward for being open and authentic is the opportunity to grow through their work, provide an environment for their staff to grow, achieve goals, and *really* help people.

As a manager or supervisor, you do many things: organize and attend meetings, draft and defend budgets, hire and supervise people. You communicate with colleagues and clients in person, on the phone, and via email. You listen to ideas and complaints, and occasionally to praise. Letters and memos emerge from your fingertips. You consider the ramifications of budget cuts and new regulations and policies. You work surrounded by people, and sometimes, when everyone else has gone home, you work alone. In fact, you may become so busy **doing** that you forget how to simply *be*.

The most important gift you can give your clients, staff, and colleagues is not merely doing what you do, but *being who you are*. The personal integrity, care, and attention you bring to your work is the foundation for everything you do. You *have* the essential characteristics to become a creative and insightful leader—your own *empowering and compassionate presence*: the unique blend of natural talents, skills, and abilities to nurture and support your own and another person's journey of healthy self-reliance and interdependence.

Your level of mindfulness and ability to be fully present with others are essential ingredients in this process. It's astonishing how often simply bringing your full attention to a situation, while offering minimal or no advice, can prompt others to develop creative and workable solutions. Of course, there are times when it's appropriate for you to be proactive—to establish guidelines and set restrictions—but when you adopt a shared-power approach, you'll be able to avoid the pitfalls and subsequent exhaustion that come with trying to micromanage your organization.

There was an old saying in farm communities: "The best fertilizer is the farmer's footsteps." Farmers used to walk around their whole farms every Sunday afternoon, often with their families. They noticed the condition of the weather, animals, fields, buildings, fences, forests, and ponds. They observed what was thriving as well as what needed tending. Along the way, they would stop frequently to examine a new type of weed sprouting up, or a limb brought down by last week's storm. They fondled the lamb born in the dark of night and drank in the beauty of the sunset. As they walked, they made mental notes of their week's to-do list. When their children accompanied them, the farmer listened to their fresh views, and pointed out interesting aspects of the farm those children would one day inherit. Wise agency leaders, like good farmers, know the importance of not merely being physically present, but staying in touch with all aspects of the agency.

In the early 1980s, Tom Peters, the author of *In Search of Excellence*, coined the term "Management by Walking Around" to apply this same caring and mindful approach to corporate management. One way in which he suggested putting this idea into practice was to use "walking around" to offer frequent and meaningful recognition to others for a job well done. In the next section, you'll learn that recognizing the natural assets of your staff and workplace is the first step in facilitating organizational transformation.

FDC Core Principles adapted for supervisors and leaders

To paraphrase three of the Core Principles of Family Development:

- All people and all families have strengths.
- The type and degree of support each family needs varies throughout their life span.
- Families and family development workers are equally important partners in the empowerment process.

Your relationships with others often reflect the way you think, act, and feel about yourself. When you make it a habit to apply the FDC Core Principle of "All people and families have strengths," you are not merely affirming the strengths you find in some people; you're *re*affirming that all people—including yourself—have strengths.

An empowerment-based relationship between a supervisor and worker shares much in common with a worker-family relationship: providing support and encouragement through difficulties, guidance with healthy risk-taking, and being a role model for others to envision themselves in the future. Here are the FDC Core Principles adapted for supervisors:

1. All supervisors, staff members, and colleagues have strengths.

2. All supervisors and staff members need and deserve support in the work environment. The type and degree of support needed varies throughout the span of employment.

3. Most successful staff members are not dependent on everyday supervision; neither are they independent in their functioning. They maintain healthy interdependence with their colleagues, supervisors, and collaborators.

4. Diversity (race, ethnicity, gender, class, family form, religion, physical and mental ability, sexual orientation) is important and valuable in the workplace. Supervisors need to develop competence in working effectively with staff who may be different from themselves, or who belong to groups not respected in our society.

5. The deficit model of supervision, in which staff members must show performance problems to receive supervision, and in which the supervisor decides what's best for staff members, is counterproductive to helping them move toward healthy self-reliance.

6. Changing to a strengths-based model of supervision requires a new way of thinking about the supervisory relationship. Supervisors cannot make this shift without corresponding changes in how they work with their department heads or more senior administrators.

7. Staff members need to implement a consistent approach in which all departments use a similar supervisory philosophy. Collaboration between departments is crucial to agency functioning, and staff that feel disempowered collaborate less successfully than those whose strengths are valued.

8. Supervisors and staff members are equally important partners in the supervision process, with each contributing important knowledge. Supervisors learn as much as staff members from the process.

9. Staff members must participate in setting their own goals and methods of achieving them. Supervisory roles include assisting staff members in setting reachable goals for their performance and self-reliance, providing access to resources needed to reach their goals, and offering encouragement.

10. Supervision is provided for staff members to reach their goals, and is not in itself a measure of success. New methods of training and evaluating supervisors and staff members are needed that measure outcomes and effectiveness of the supervisory partnership, not just the number of contacts.

11. For staff members to feel valued and committed, the supervisory system must shift from a power-over to a shared-power paradigm. Supervisors have power because they participate in the distribution of valued resources (status, promotion, recognition). They can then use those resources to support staff members, rather than exert power over them.

How the family development approach aligns with models of effective supervision

The growth of our economy has created a flurry of interest in leadership development. You probably receive information about leadership seminars, webinars, podcasts, and conferences that promise you'll leave these sessions able to more effectively "manage" any type of situation or employee. You can read books written by successful businesspeople who've led large companies with impressive results, or textbooks by scholars who've studied leadership theory. Learning about the various approaches to supervision and leadership can help you stay informed about helpful and creative ways to motivate and negotiate everyday challenges. But attending a conference, then introducing the latest management technique for just a few weeks, can be confusing to staff members and, over time, erode their trust in your commitment to meaningful and enduring change. A good way to begin developing your own workable model of effective supervision is to consider current theories that support the underlying philosophy of your organization, then take a hard look at your own leadership style.

Lawrence Shulman, a former professor and Dean at the State University of New York at Buffalo School of Social Work, suggested that the traditional, authoritarian model of supervision fosters a "transactional" (cause-effect) relationship between a supervisor and staff. In research done with social workers, Shulman discovered that relationships are interactions that result in what he terms "reciprocal influences" occurring between a staff member, a supervisor, and the agency. He proposes that effective supervision is best represented as an "interactional" model that incorporates the separate yet interconnected relationships between supervisor, staff member, and agency. His model of *interactional supervision* looks like this:

Shulman's Interactional Model of Supervision

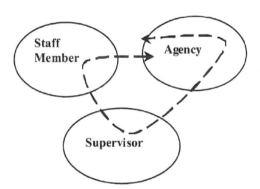

Shulman's Interactional Model of Supervision recognizes that supervisors have separate, yet interconnected, relationships with both workers and families.[10] In family development, a supervisor is an important partner in the family-worker relationship in two capacities: working with their agency to develop and offer services for families to achieve healthy self-reliance, and helping workers overcome obstacles in order to provide meaningful support for families. The model of interactional supervision aligns well with the following Core Principle of Family Development and its adaptation for supervisors and leaders.

Core Principle of Family Development #8

Families and family development workers are equally important partners in the empowerment process, with each contributing important knowledge. Workers learn as much as families from the process.

Core Principle of Family Development #8 adapted for supervisors and leaders

Supervisors and staff members are equally important partners in the supervision process, with each contributing important knowledge. Supervisors learn as much as staff members from the process.

In everyday tasks, the differences in use between transactional and interactional supervision might appear subtle, but the impact on developing empowering relationships with staff members can be profound. For example, a competent and caring worker may come to you asking for a pay raise after a program budget has been finalized. Using a transactional approach to supervision, you might simply tell them that the budget had already been finalized, thus their request couldn't be considered. However, if you were to use an interactional approach, you would demonstrate as much concern for their request as for other items included in the program budget. You would then respond by learning more about their needs, explaining budget projections, considering creative options to collaborate on meeting their goals, and possibly even including a raise.

The reality of considering a pay raise in accordance with the finalized budget might still result in your not being able to offer it at this time. However, using an interactional approach to supervision, your response to this situation recognized the value and importance of the request. In this way, you will have maintained a healthy partnership with this staff member.

Another model of supervision consistent with the family development approach is *developmental supervision*. The goal of developmental supervision is to help workers build and enhance their capacities for responsibility and healthy interdependence with families and colleagues in their work environment. In their model of developmental supervision, Glickman, Gordon, and Ross-Gordon propose that there are four basic approaches: direction, education, collaboration, and support.[11] The key to effective supervision, in their view, is a supervisor's ability to use the four approaches flexibly in working with individuals and groups of workers. For example, as a worker demonstrates skills and competency in accomplishing tasks that require greater levels of autonomy and responsibility, the supervisor adjusts their supervisory approach from directive to supportive. But the supervisor also stands ready to assess and alter their approach as the process develops. Using this model, the supervisory role resembles that of a coach, facilitator, mentor, and resource person.

The family development approach and developmental supervision model share a key guiding principle: *the purpose of the relationship is not just its outcome, but that the quality of the relationship is equally important.*

Comparing the roles of family development workers with the four approaches of developmental supervision

The following chart compares the Roles of Family Development Workers with the four approaches of developmental supervision:

Roles of Family Development Workers to help families achieve healthy self-reliance and interdependence with their community.	Roles of a supervisor using the Four Approaches of Developmental Supervision to help workers balance autonomy and responsibility
1. To help families create their own long and short-term goals. 2. To help families gain access to the services they need to reach these goals.	To provide an appropriate level of direction for a worker to develop healthy autonomy. High need Low need **Direction**
3. To help families assess their own strengths and needs, reflect critically on how they arrived where they are, and determine what will help them move toward self-reliance.	To provide necessary information needed for a worker to act with responsibility. High need Low need **Education (Information)**
4. To encourage families to develop their own strengths as they move toward their goals including practicing needed skills.	To provide clarification, encouragement, and guidance based on the assumption that a worker knows best what changes need to be made. High need Low need **Collaboration**
5. To help families restore their sense of self-respect, self-reliance and hope. 6. To help families reclaim their dreams of a better life.	To assist workers with assessment and planning in a way that supports the worker individually, and at the organizational level. High need Low need **Support**

Reflective leadership

Reflective leadership is a way of approaching the work of being a leader by leading one's life with presence and personal mastery. Learning to be present, to be aware and attentive to our experiences and interactions with people throughout the day, is the focus of reflective leadership.[12] This is also a focus of the family development approach and empowerment-based leadership.

From our past experiences, most of us can think of someone we would describe as being an effective leader. Think about some words or phrases you would use to describe that individual. These may include:

- Communicates a shared vision

- Confident
- Can do attitude
- Facilitates and compromises
- Flexible/adaptive
- Listens
- Motivates staff
- Provides support and encouragement
- Respects staff opinions and feedback
- Sets clear goals
- Shares achievements
- Trusts employees
- Uses humor

To embody all these characteristics is a tall order for any leader but certainly something to strive for. While effectiveness as a leader is often measured quantitatively, almost all these qualities relate to managing relationships with others, sometimes called "soft skills." It's our skill in connecting with, guiding and mentoring staff that make those quantitative goals achievable.

Reflective leadership is characterized by three important skills: self-awareness, careful observation, and flexible responses.[13]

- *Self-awareness* refers to knowing your own unique gifts and talents, along with your biases and limitations. It's sometimes easier to list our shortcomings than all our positive aspects. There are tools, such as Strengths Finder, that can help you reflect on your positive attributes.
- *Careful observation* requires leaders to be skilled at listening and figuring out the meaning behind what they see and hear. This can include noticing behavior, tone of voice, body language, and reactions and asking yourself: Why might this be happening? Listening fully and reflectively is a skill that takes practice. However, it can provide important insights into how to work effectively with others.
- *Flexible responses* require leaders to know the personal styles of their staff, how they work best, and what motivates them. Leaders can then approach each staff member in a way that reflects their individual needs, strengths, and address areas for improvement as needed.

Reflective leaders set goals, provide feedback, encourage, inspire, and promote self-monitoring. They draw upon the individual's strengths to offer a variety of approaches to accomplish their work, while continually clarifying and extending ideas. This may sound like a lot of work you don't have time for, but it can actually save you time in the long run, as staff members build confidence in their tasks and require less oversight.

So, why is it important to reflect? According to Professor Patricia Castelli of Lawrence Technical University in Michigan, leaders who are reflective can bring about improvements in employee well-being, engagement, and performance. Reflective leadership can also result in improved organizational performance. Castelli suggests six behaviors that can help to develop reflective leaders:[14]

1. *Value open communication.* Activities such as informally checking in and regular meetings that encourage open channels of communication provide opportunities for staff to share ideas and ask questions to clarify their roles.

2. *Build self-esteem and confidence.* Delegating responsibilities, offering professional development, and recognizing accomplishments are examples of strategies that build confidence in staff.

3. *Challenge beliefs and assumptions.* "It's always worked like this" or "We do it this way" are common phrases in the workplace. Honest self-reflection requires recognition of our own blind spots, an openness to alternatives, and willingness to change.

4. *Create a safe environment that promotes trust.* Showing integrity through consistency and modeling what you want to see, along with valuing different opinions, demonstrates to staff that you care about their contributions.

5. *Help others understand how their work relates to the achievement of organizational goals.* Looking at the big picture, help staff to recognize how their role in the workplace contributes to the overall mission.

6. *Respect diversity.* This includes respecting the customs and values of others, promoting inclusiveness, and being sensitive to individual differences.

Taggart and Wilson (2005) developed a reflective thinking model using these steps:[15]

1. Identify a problem, challenge, or dilemma.

2. Step back and look at the problem from a third-person perspective. This involves observation, data gathering, reflection, and consideration of the principles you value.

3. Ask what has worked for you in the past in similar situations, and what is different now?

4. Identify and test solutions, then review the actions taken and any consequences.

5. Do you feel the situation was successfully resolved? If not, repeat this process.

Here are some additional strategies to develop reflective thinking, some of which you may not have considered[16]:

- Use visual art. Draw whatever you're thinking without using words.
- Spend time on a creative endeavor. This can rest your mind and re-energize you.
- Physical activity can help you to better understand your body.
- Spend time with people who bring out the best in you.
- Journal writing can also promote self-awareness. Taking a few minutes each day to write about your feelings and experiences can help you process your inner wisdom.

Leaders who practice reflective thinking are taking the first steps toward being a reflective leader. This is a process that can transform the culture of your workplace into one that reflects and reinforces the eleven principles of family development adapted for leaders and promotes empowerment-based leadership.

Two other leadership styles that align with the family development approach

The term "servant-leader" was coined in 1970 by the late Robert Greenleaf, who spent many years as Director of Management Research at AT&T and as a lecturer at MIT. He defined "servant-leader" as an individual who aspires to lead through service to others. In 1996, Don Frick and Larry Spears published a book entitled *On Becoming a Servant Leader: The Private Writings of Robert K. Greenleaf,*[17] which defines a servant-leader as someone who responds to their desire to serve others by forming a conscious aspiration to lead. Greenleaf proposed that servant-leaders approach relationships with others, whether professional or personal, from an ethical base of commitment and empathy for the physical, emotional, and spiritual well-being of others.

It's easy to see how the qualities of servant-leaders are reflected in the roles and responsibilities of supervisors and leaders of family-serving organizations today. Those working in the "human services" profession, broadly defined as anyone involved with the welfare and well-being of others, have opportunities to see how service to others influences and enriches their own lives. In recent years, some large corporations have included the concept of servant-leadership in restructuring their organizations, so that business leaders can witness the impact their efforts have on the customers they serve.

At first glance, reading the terms "family development" and "servant-leadership" out of context, it's easy to understand why they can be awkward to define and describe. Their literal definitions don't translate neatly into clear meanings or standard practice. The terms are descriptive rather than prescriptive and provide a broader context for how to *be* an effective leader, rather than on some technique that allows us to *do* it.

In the family development approach, workers learn that the conventional wisdom of providing services to help families achieve "self-sufficiency" has not substantially helped families decrease their dependence on assistance programs. Similarly, you may relate to the qualities of servant-leadership, yet feel challenged to revise your own leadership theory that defines a leader by the scope and level of power and control to be exerted over others. Leadership can be an undesirable job, even on the best of days. A solid grounding in your own philosophy of leadership will help guide and support you in making decisions that underpin the ethical "non-negotiables" of a program or organization, especially during times of misfortune and crisis.

Another leadership model, *connective leadership*, developed by Harvard organizational psychologist Jean Lipman-Blumen stresses the importance of leadership in uniting resources to achieve common goals through shared vision.[18] She argues that there is a need for a fundamental shift in leadership as organizations and nations enter a new period of development that she calls the "Connective Era." As technology has advanced, there is a true "global village" for anyone with Internet access. Lipman-Blumen believes that leaders will play a pivotal role in connecting the opposing forces of global interdependence and diversity. She predicts that the changing conditions of leadership will affect all national, organizational, and community leaders by requiring them to respond more quickly, decisively, and collaboratively. The role of a leader in the Connective Era, she wrote, "will be to unite and share power with those they lead, but also to collaborate well with other leaders."

We have seen these predictions come to fruition. Connective leaders are those who demonstrate leadership by, for example:

- Building cohesive relationships with others based on seeking out mutual problems as well as goals
- Reaching out to former opponents to help create grander visions for the greater community
- Valuing diversity as a necessary component in opportunity
- Embracing the concept of shared power as a way to empower others

The Core Principles of Family Development and the qualities of connective leaders both focus on the relationship between interdependence, diversity, and empowerment. The table below describes some of the ways in which the FDC Core Principles correspond with the qualities and actions of a connective leader:

Core Principles of Family Development	Qualities and Actions of a *Connective Leader*
1. All people and all families have strengths. 2. The type and degree of support each family needs varies throughout their life span.	Builds cohesive relationships with others based on seeking out mutual concerns as well as goals
7. Families need coordinated services in which all agencies they work with use a similar approach. Collaboration at the local, state, and federal levels is crucial to effective family development.	Reaches out to former opponents to help with grander visions of the greater Community
4. Diversity (race, ethnicity, gender, class, family form, religion, physical and mental ability, age, sexual orientation) is an important and valuable reality in our society.	Sees diversity as a valuable and necessary component of opportunity
11. For families to move out of dependency, helping systems must shift from a power-over to a shared-power paradigm. Human service workers have power (which they may not recognize) because they participate in the distribution of valued resources. Workers can use that power to work with families.	Shares power as the way to empower others

A connective leader doesn't spend a great deal of time glued to their computer screen at their desk. Rather, they spend most of each day actively involved in the organization—leading staff meetings, courting new service partners, consulting with collaborators, and advocating with policymakers. In short, they're always making connections. If you recognize yourself by this description as a connective leader, hopefully you'll be pleased to read that the full pace you keep up each day is grounded in an exemplary leadership style.

Theories such as servant-leadership and connective leadership are conceptual models—ideas developed within a philosophical framework to explain similar and different ways that leaders respond to the calling and challenge of leading others. Most leadership models attempt to explain the motivations and actions of leaders by highlighting their strengths and diminishing their limitations. No model is perfect. You may feel that some aspects of your leadership style align with multiple models. Leadership models, at their most basic level, are informed attempts to identify and explain common elements of complex leadership behavior. At their grandest level, leadership models reveal what our larger culture believes to be the most significant challenges, struggles, and triumphs of leadership at a given point in time.

What is your leadership style?

If a friend or colleague were to ask you to describe what type of leader you are, how would you respond? If you're like most leaders, you'd probably start by describing some qualities you feel you have or relaying what others have told you about yourself. It's possible that the qualities you describe may not exactly match how your staff perceives you. It's also likely that your leadership style will change with time and experience, and may vary from one situation to another.

In *The Connective Edge: Leading in an Interdependent World*,[19] Lipman-Blumen defines the essentials of effective leadership as a set of interpersonal and management skills and abilities we paraphrase here and present in the context of family support organizations. These are:

- To attract, inspire, and retain family support professionals in times of social, political, and economic change
- To collaboratively design and implement programs that meet families' complex and changing needs
- To build and develop their organization's capacity for cultural competence, teamwork, innovation, and outcome-based collaboration
- To nurture, support, collaborate, solve problems, and make decisions with family support staff using shared power

Lipman-Blumen describes nine leadership styles that incorporate these essentials focused on the strengths of individuals who serve as leaders. These descriptions, outlined in the following table, should help you think about and define your own leadership style.

Leadership Style	Lipman-Blumen's Description: A Leader Who ...
Intrinsic	Focuses on mastery of skills and consistent, high-quality work performance to help workers understand that satisfaction comes from doing their best
Competitive	Leads efforts toward an external standard of excellence or the common goal, or mission, of the organization
Power	Achieves results by organizing and directing people, delegating tasks, and allocating resources (often used to manage crisis situations)
Collaborative	Stresses relationships, seeks to resolve conflicts, and advance shared visions
Contributory	Promotes the organization's goals by identifying with the people (families, clients, customers) being helped
Vicarious	Encourages and supports accomplishments of others as if they were their own
Personal	Accentuates the physical, emotional, and intuitive qualities (charisma) in their role as leader to persuade others to act
Social	Cultivates helpful personal relationships and networks within and outside the organization to achieve goals
Entrusting	Selects staff members with the necessary skills to make decisions, then places trust in them and provides adequate freedom to complete a task

Using Lipman-Blumen's descriptions, write the leadership styles you use most often for each group below (you can indicate more than one style for category):

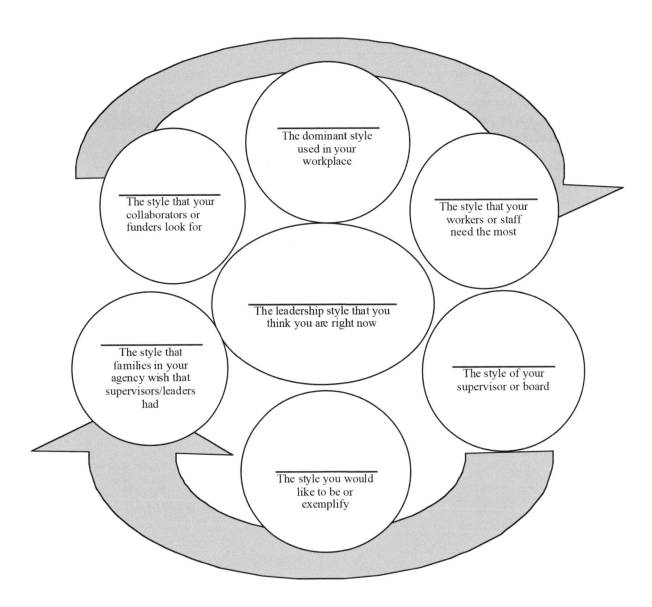

The dominant style used in your workplace

The style that your collaborators or funders look for

The style that your workers or staff need the most

The leadership style that you think you are right now

The style that families in your agency wish that supervisors/leaders had

The style of your supervisor or board

The style you would like to be or exemplify

When you've completed this exercise, take a few minutes to reflect on these questions:

- *What can I learn about myself as a leader by identifying the types of leadership styles I use with different groups?*

- *Do I use the same leadership style(s) with most groups or are there variations?*

While some leaders adhere to a single style, most leaders incorporate aspects of several different styles into their approach. Many work environments require that leaders adapt their personal leadership styles to conform to overall organizational culture. An insight you gain from recognizing your leadership style is that you can become more consciously aware of qualities your staff and colleagues already recognize in you!

A leadership style works well for you if it "fits" your personality and allows you to recognize and develop your strengths while maintaining mutually respectful relationships with staff members and colleagues. If you try to adopt a leadership style that doesn't work well for you, you may experience conflict between your "leader" personality at work, and your "true" personality that appears in less-public situations.

If you want to modify your leadership style to an approach more compatible with your true personality or work environment, begin to act in ways that reflect the style you want to have. If you want to be a more trusting leader, begin by identifying those who can be trusted to make good decisions. Then, work with them to develop and complete a project. Provide the freedom and resources for them to do the job well, and resist the urge to take over if they become stuck or confused. While you'll need to encourage them, and set clear expectations and deadlines, their ultimate success will reflect the extent to which you've trusted in their abilities, as well as how successfully the project has reached its goal.

Leaders as organizational role models

Some relationships provide natural "role model" opportunities, such as parenting, teaching, and counseling. The relationship between a leader and a staff member can also be a role modeling opportunity. Daniel Goleman, Harvard psychologist and author of *Working with Emotional Intelligence*,[20] uses the term "emotional intelligence" to describe the personal capacities and skills that contribute to the healthy growth and development of workers and leaders. The application of emotional intelligence in the workplace helps you to better assess people, understand how relationships develop, and prevent power struggles and negative judgment. Goleman identified five competencies of emotional intelligence:

- *Self-awareness*: the ability to recognize and understand your moods, emotions, and drives, as well as their effect on others.
- *Self-regulation*: the ability to control or redirect disruptive impulses and moods, or to suspend judgment and think before acting.
- *Motivation*: a passion to work for reasons that go beyond money or status; the ability to pursue goals with energy and persistence.
- *Empathy*: the ability to understand the emotional makeup of other people, and to treat people according to their emotional needs.
- *Social Skills*: the ability to manage relationships in order to build networks, find common ground, and build rapport.

Goleman suggests we can develop our capacities for self-awareness, self-regulation, motivation, empathy, and social skills throughout adulthood. How do we do this? We use role models—people whose actions we carefully observe—to learn new ways to think, feel, and act. Below are some ways that you can model emotional intelligence in your relationships with staff and colleagues.

Self-awareness

The distance between a thought, a feeling, and an action can be mere milliseconds. Our bodies are naturally equipped with involuntary reflexes and a complex nervous system to protect us from physical harm. Emotions are natural responses that protect us from psychological stress. Developing greater awareness of your emotions and moods requires taking time to think and feel *before* you act.

Empowerment-based relationships flourish when each person brings their full *self*-awareness (thoughts, feelings, and actions) to the partnership. Leaders can model self-awareness by sharing how their emotions affect them (e.g., "I'm not feeling very energetic today") and acknowledging how their moods may affect others (e.g., "I didn't get much sleep last night, so I'm not my usual self").

Self-regulation

In most organizations, leaders are expected to hold things together when everything seems to be falling apart. Some leaders even say they do their best work under pressure, and become more focused and energized during a crisis. Inevitably, all leaders have experiences that test the limits of their coping skills both personally and professionally.

Being a leader when the budget balances, programs are successful, and staff are content and productive can be exhilarating. But being a leader when funding has been cut, programs are failing, and staff are being cut is agonizing. Especially during those times when you feel stressed and less in control, it's important to regain balance between your work as a leader and your life as a partner, parent, and friend (among other roles you may have). You need to take good care of yourself—physically, emotionally, socially, and spiritually—to be an effective leader. Furthermore, the way you take care of yourself sets an example for others.

Motivation

You probably think of motivation as something you do for others more than something you do for yourself. Today's media portray political and corporate leaders as motivational speakers; thus, we can easily be taken in by the delivery of their message as opposed to its content. How does a leader model self-motivation? The first part of the answer is, by making the effort. The second part of the answer is, by getting results. You model self-motivation for others whenever your efforts produce their intended results.

The best part about modeling self-motivation is that making the effort doesn't only require getting results in the workplace. You can model self-motivation in a multitude of other ways: by enrolling and completing an adult education course, by taking a few lessons to learn a new sport or hobby, or by attending the *Empowerment Skill for Leaders* course, just to name a few.

Think of a person in your life who you look up to as a role model. At some level, their self-motivation was a model or inspiration to you. As a leader, you have a unique opportunity to motivate others in these direct and indirect ways.

Empathy

In human service professions, *empathy* is the guiding principle behind the work we do. The continuum of emotions that describe feelings we have about the misfortune of others typically begins with apathy (a lack of feeling for another's troubles), moves to sympathy (sharing similar feelings about someone's misfortune), and finally reaches empathy (acknowledging what the situation might feel like if it were to happen to you). Leaders model empathy through their openness to learn ways that their position in the organization limits their awareness of other's viewpoints and experiences.

From a family worker's viewpoint, the challenges of offering family support may be in sharp contrast with how a leader might see the same situation. There's the saying that empathy means "putting ourselves in another's shoes." When you model empathy, you not only put on another's shoes, you "walk their walk" to learn where it hurts, and then offer what you can to comfort and help.

Social skills

In FDC training, workers learn a variety of useful communication techniques to develop mutually respectful relationships with families. They practice skills such as active listening, door openers to facilitate discussion, paraphrasing, feedback, "I" messages, and conflict resolution. A leader who in turn uses these techniques in their interactions with a worker sends a clear message of respect for the supervisor-worker relationship.

Leaders also model social skills by helping workers understand the organization's philosophy and approach to interagency collaboration. Despite tremendous progress in shifting the paradigm of deficit-based family assistance to empowerment-based family support, your agency will continue to face challenges in negotiating relationships with new and existing collaborators. You also can model empowerment-based communication techniques to other leaders and staff involved in collaborations with your agency.

As a leader, it can be difficult to live up to the expectations of those who see you as a personal or professional role model. Here are some ideas to help you think realistically about being a role model:

- *No role model is perfect.* Every admirable historic, political, or social leader has had flaws. Role models are fallible human beings who constantly strive to align their actions with their beliefs and values.

- *Role models are needed through all stages of life.* Today's fast-paced, technologically isolating world offers few opportunities to learn from direct experience. Role models who have managed their way through the many stages of life can have valuable experiences and lessons to share.

- *Role models are everywhere.* Think about your own role models and their "specialties": your friend with incredible patience, your colleague who always comes up with new ideas, or your staff member who consistently maintains warm and trusting relationships with families.

- *Role modeling is more art than science.* Good role models use their talents to inspire others through their experiences, perceptions, personal judgments, instincts, and creativity.

Recognizing the natural assets of staff members

When things are going well at your agency, it's easy to focus on the unique assets of your staff, who work hard to make the community a safe and healthy place, and are committed to helping families. The natural assets of your staff—dedication, creativity, optimism, and persistence—are qualities that help people stay focused on serving the mission of the organization, especially during times when funding and other so-called "fixed" assets are in flux.

An agency director who participated in an FDC Leadership Curriculum focus group said:

> *You have this sense of the philosophy and then it is so easy to fall off the wagon, to not incorporate it on a daily basis. As a supervisor, often the family worker is talking to you about a crisis situation, and you come at it in your crisis mode. It's hard to stop and regroup and remember to ask that one question: "What is going right?"*

Recognizing the natural strengths and abilities of staff members and the workplace is different from counting the fixed assets of your agency, such as vehicles, furnishings, or equipment. When you combine the natural assets of staff with a common purpose and goal, you create a chemistry that brings out a wonderful mixture of strengths and abilities.

One of the most important skills you need as a leader is the ability to help workers identify and build on their strengths. Every interaction you have with staff members provides an opportunity to reflect their strengths back to them. You can enhance your ability to work with staff by focusing on their strengths and affirming that each worker brings valuable knowledge and experience to the agency.

Working from the strengths perspective doesn't mean you ignore real problems. It means you deeply believe that all workers have strengths and that they can use these strengths to solve problems and meet goals. Even traits that appear negative usually have at least some strengths behind them. Your job is to help workers recognize their strengths and find healthy ways to build on them. You'll find that focusing on strengths can become a positive, affirming way of looking at the world.

Aligning your leadership vision with the mission of the organization

The third step in transforming your workplace through empowerment-based leadership is to align your vision with your organization's mission. Formal mission statements are usually concise (less than 25 words), consistent in format (i.e., what, for whom, how, and to what outcome), and broad in scope. Even if your leadership within the organization is limited, you know the products and services your organization provides, the individuals or families it serves, how that service is delivered, and the overall outcome it seeks to achieve. New employee orientation packets and customer-service training always include a copy of the mission statement, and many organizations now display their mission statements in public areas such as elevators and waiting rooms.

In today's ever-changing social and political climate, a mission statement affirms the stability of an organization's role in the community. Leaders and staff members may come and go, but a mission statement endures as part of an organization's history. Aligning your leadership vision with the mission of your organization is critical to maintaining the stability that both staff and families need. Use the space below to write your organization's mission statement.

Your Organization's Mission Statement

Product(s)/service(s) provided: _____

Whom the organization serves: _____

How it serves: _____

Desired outcome: _____

Or, write the mission statement here: _____

_____

_____

_____

Imagine that you need services and are approaching your organization for the first time? What direct and unspoken messages would you receive?

In addition to a mission statement, there are many ways in which agencies send positive and inspiring messages to families that reflect the organization's philosophy. For example, a worker who recognizes and affirms a family's strengths is sending a positive philosophical message of mutual respect. Yet there are messages that are detrimental to helping families achieve healthy self-reliance. Here are three examples of organizational practices that send *negative* philosophical messages to families:

Policies/practices that send a negative message to families	How this makes a family member feel
An agency requires a family member to complete the same form every time they use a service.	"The agency doesn't trust that I'll give the same information each time, or that I'll keep them up to date on changes."
"Intervention" programs that provide intensive family support, and services that end as soon as the family works through an immediate crisis.	"In order to get services I need, I have to have an ongoing problem or else the agency won't help me."
Agency assessment forms focus the family-worker relationship on resolving "problems" instead of recognizing strengths, and developing and achieving goals.	"Good things I might have done in the past count for little, because I am asking for help today. Doing what it takes to get help, I end up feeling worthless as a person."

If your organization currently uses policies or practices such as those listed above, don't feel immediately disheartened that families are receiving services based on a deficit-based model of support. In some cases, these policies and practices are necessary to safeguard confidentiality and maintain accurate record-keeping.

No matter what leadership role you have in your organization, you can help transform your workplace through empowerment-based leadership. Your leadership vision doesn't require that you solve every problem overnight. Empowerment-based leadership is a process of developing and implementing a vision that provides the same levels of support to workers that families receive.

In organizations that use the family development model of family support, workers develop relationships based on identifying strengths, building trust and mutual respect, and helping families' goals of healthy self-reliance. As a supervisor or leader of an organization, you can support workers and staff members by:

1. Making a commitment to building partnerships based on shared power
2. Recognizing the natural strengths and abilities of the staff members
3. Aligning your leadership vision with the mission of the organization and the messages it sends
4. Setting and achieving short-term goals to transform your vision into reality

The last step above is a critical one for sharing your vision with staff members in tangible and demonstrable ways. In beginning to actualize your leadership vision, ask yourself:

- What goals do I want to achieve?
- In what ways can I support my staff members and develop mutually respectful relationships?

A great way to develop or clarify your leadership vision is to work with staff in setting a goal and preparing a plan to achieve a mutually agreeable outcome. Below is a list of goals that supervisors and leaders have told us they would like to achieve with their staff members. Read through the list (or use it to develop your own short-term goals for using empowerment-based leadership in your organization). Then review the list, and place a "√" next to three outcomes that you would like to work on with your staff members or co-workers. Below the list is some space for any additional goals you may wish to include.

Goals for Workplace Empowerment

_____ Appreciate each staff member's unique talents and abilities

_____ Help staff members put new skills to use

_____ Provide orientation and training to enhance job performance

_____ Provide resources needed to do a job well (e.g., time, equipment, supplies, information)

_____ Develop timeframes for getting work done

_____ Support and help workers in prioritizing tasks

_____ Reprioritize needs and tasks to accomplish time-sensitive work

_____ Give regular feedback and encouragement to staff members

_____ Support when unanticipated problems or situations occur

_____ Get input and feedback from staff members and co-workers

_____ Give praise and recognition as goals are achieved

_____ Provide a balance of challenge and routine in job tasks

_____ Develop a sense of community within the organization

_____ Recognize ways that individuals and teams make an important contribution

_____ Develop ways for co-workers to support each other

_____ Develop new working relationships with other teams or departments

_____ _____

_____ _____

_____ _____

_____ _____

Now that you've identified three potential goals to discuss with staff, consider one that can be achieved in relatively few steps. In developing a mutual goal for workplace empowerment, it's critical to take suggestions and feedback from staff members who will be directly involved in achieving the outcome.

Once the group has selected a goal, perform the following steps:

1. Working together identify the specific steps and time frame required to make consistent progress in achieving the goal.
2. Create a list of the natural assets and strengths the group has that would contribute to your success.
3. Talk about and record any concerns you or staff members might have about achieving the goal.
4. Generate a list of available services and resources needed, including names, addresses, and phone numbers.
5. Finally, set a date when you will get together again to review your progress.

To convert what you've just read about into a working plan, you can use a form such as the one on the next page:

Workplace Empowerment Plan for ...

_____
agency or program name

Today's date: _____

Supervisor and Staff Members involved in this workplace empowerment process: _____

_____

_____

Short-term goal:

_____

_____

Steps leading to this goal:

Steps the supervisor will take and when:

_____

_____

_____

Steps workers and staff members will take and when:

_____

_____

_____

Natural assets and strengths (staff members, supervisor, co-workers, and others in the organization):

_____

_____

_____

Concerns (staff members, supervisor, co-workers, and others in the organization):

_____

_____

_____

Services and resources available (including names, addresses, phone numbers, etc.):

_____

_____

_____

Date, time, and place set to review progress: _____

Names of people who will attend progress meeting: _____

The Workplace Empowerment Plan is an adaptation of the Family Development Plan used by thousands of families and workers to develop, set, and achieve goals of healthy self-reliance. After you complete your first plan, remember to give everyone copies. When you meet again, use the plan as a reference and, if necessary, revise it until the goal is achieved.

Transforming your workplace may sometimes seem like a lofty ideal requiring complex and sophisticated plans—along with "the moon and sun in perfect alignment"—to achieve your desired results. Transformation is actually a process we witness every day in nature, as dawn brings light to energize the earth's creatures, daylight guides them through their goals for the day, and night restores tired minds and hearts through rest in anticipation of another day.

Assessing the level of empowerment in your workplace

If a colleague from another organization were to tell you that "morale at our agency is at an all-time low," you could probably guess at the level of empowerment in that workplace, whether or not you knew how much morale they'd had before. In assessing the level of empowerment in your workplace, you may need to go beyond finding out how staff feel about current working conditions. Periodically, you may want to assess what your intuition is telling you about how staff members might think or feel about a given situation. Your organization may be committed to providing services according to the family development approach, but there may be front-line workers (as well as supervisors and leaders) who are not convinced the paradigm shift required for this approach will result in long-term, sustainable benefits.

In *Empowerment Skills for Family Workers*, empowerment is defined as "a dynamic process through which families and individuals reach their own goals. No one can "empower" someone else." Despite this fact, there are ways you can enhance your staff's capacity for personal empowerment. For example, you can provide time and resources for them to attend FDC and other professional development training programs that develop and nurture their capacity for empowerment.

When FDC first began credentialing workers, far-reaching federal legislation affected family-serving organizations in profound new ways. The Government Performance Results Act, and the Personal Responsibility and Work Opportunity Reconciliation Act (also called "welfare reform")—both of which were enacted in the mid-1990s—resulted in stricter eligibility requirements and outcomes-based accountability for social service programs that receive federal funding. As a result, professionals trained in empowerment-based family support are faced with a dilemma when the services a family needs may not be allowed or approved because of funding regulations. For example, workers can feel torn between their belief in empowering families and the need to enforce organizational policies or governmental regulations that might result in denial or withdrawal of a family's services. There are similar situations today regarding immigration, work requirements, and other restrictions. Another factor is trying to manage large caseloads and multiple work responsibilities without having enough time to implement the best practices known to be more effective. Budget cuts can mean fewer staff doing the same amount of work.

This can leave workers experiencing "dissonance," a state of mind that occurs when a person experiences conflict between two competing belief or value systems. To reconcile the conflict, workers might try to tell themselves there's a valid reason for acting in a way contrary to their beliefs, or try to minimize the importance or impact of their actions. Family workers might try to resolve the conflict by:

1. Shifting to the belief that empowerment-based support should be provided to families only under circumstances deemed worthy

2. Performing work duties with a "by the book" attitude, and feeling stressed about having to act in a way that conflicts with their values

3. Becoming trapped in a "submission and aggression" relationship loop with families

4. A combination of any or all the above; these conflicting feelings may have an impact on you, as well as on co-workers and their own families

As a supervisor or leader, you're similarly affected by organizational constraints and demands. You may feel disempowered by the restrictions and regulations that limit your organization's ability to provide comprehensive family support services. You may feel frustrated that programs providing empowerment-based support for families, at the onset, require an additional and complicated investment of staff time and resources.

In the steps we've outlined to transform your workplace, assessing your own level of empowerment is crucial to maintaining open and authentic relationships with staff members. At the end of this chapter, there's an activity for independent learning to help you explore your ideas about the level of empowerment that influence the purpose and goal of a helping relationship. Once you identify your ideas, you might want to compare them with staff members and families in your organization. Comparing similarities and differences in your perception of empowerment with others can help you respond to families, staff members, and funders more empathically, and maintain mutually respectful and effective working relationships.

Building your agency's capacity for transformation

The book *The Change Leader's Roadmap: How to Navigate Your Organization's Transformation*, by Linda Ackerman Anderson and Dean Anderson,[21] outlines three types of organizational change:

- Developmental
- Transitional
- Transformational

The authors describe *developmental* change in organizations as a broad-based organizational effort to develop skills and competencies of staff members so they can perform their jobs more effectively, or with greater impact on productivity and outcomes. For example, staff in-service training to learn how to use a new outcome-measurement software program involves developmental change for your organization.

Transitional change involves combining efforts across the organization that might affect multiple levels of operation and administration. This type of change might be intended to replace outdated modes of operation or management with new and improved techniques. An example of transitional change is when an organization restructures departments and responsibilities for program outcomes from a traditional supervisor-leader management approach to one focused on team-based accountability.

Transformational change is an effort to fundamentally and profoundly alter the purpose and foundations of an organization that affects employees, customers, competitors, and even the wider culture. Organizational transformation is an ongoing process that delves beneath the surface of normal organizational practices and requires attentiveness to the impact of change itself on the organization.

Because the scope of transformational change in an organization is usually so sweeping and far-reaching, leaders who undertake this type of change can expect strong staff reactions, reservations, and perhaps even resistance. At the onset of transformational change, the attitudes, feelings, and behaviors of staff members—and possibly some key advisors and stakeholders—may be motivated by a deep-seated fear of change. By taking the time and effort to build your organization's capacity for transformation, you can help address and dispel often-valid assumptions that systemic change benefits those with positional power in the organization and harms those with less power.

Every leader in your organization, from frontline supervisor to the CEO, can play a critical role in transforming the workplace through empowerment-based leadership. Each leader has a "sphere of influence": those you supervise and lead, and your program, department, organization, region, or state. Here are some ways in which you, as leader, can collaborate in building your organization's capacity for transformation:

- *Prepare your organization for transformative change in ways that help all staff members appreciate and support one another.* Frontline family workers are impacted by the shift to empowerment-based relationships with families in different ways than staff members in areas such as accounting or human resources. Find out what concerns your staff members have as they anticipate changes in their organizational duties and relationships. Talk with other leaders, and introduce transformative change at an incremental pace.

- Recognize that although broad-based organizational change is usually planned and expected, developmental and transitional changes often occur at the same time as transformative change. Most organizations replace and update equipment on an ongoing basis through line-item budget allocations. Sometimes, new programs incorporate training funds for staff to learn specialized skills or technology. Timing is a key factor when introducing any type of change in your organization. It's important to consider the types of organizational change that a department or program is already experiencing *before* introducing a new one. Then, you can orchestrate transformative change without forcing departments or programs to "catch up" or compete with colleagues from another department.

- *Support staff members in reflecting on the process of organizational change.* Some of the fear and resistance you observe in staff members may be a natural response to change and loss, not necessarily a rejection of the process of positive change for the organization. For example, some organizations have messaging systems to direct incoming calls. The decision whether to use technology to answer the phones or an actual person can be a philosophical as well as a financial one.

- *Provide opportunities for staff members to share their ideas and feelings about what's working well and what isn't.* They often have a valuable perspective about areas affected by transformative change that can only be seen from their vantage point. When you respond with compassion and practical assistance during the process of change, you provide support toward a critical collective capacity for transformation.

"Talking the talk" and "walking the walk" of a family development workplace

In FDC training, workers learn that to "walk the walk"—and not merely "talk the talk"—means to become actively involved in helping their organization apply the philosophy and practices of family development in concrete ways. In a family development workplace, everyone benefits from shared knowledge and expertise. Leadership requires making tough choices, especially when it comes to discontinuing programs, cutting budgets, or laying off staff members. And even after you've made a decision, you often need to reassess its impact on families, staff, and the organization itself.

To both "talk the talk" and "walk the walk" as a leader, you need to continuously reassess opportunities and challenges. Using principles of empowerment-based assessment, you won't need to continually rationalize or re-strategize every decision. When you make decisions based on ongoing assessment that focuses on families and staff strengths, you're using empowerment-based assessment.

In *Empowerment Skills for Family Workers*, these seven basic principles of empowerment-oriented assessment emphasize that using ongoing assessment that's strengths-based helps families decide on their own goals and how to reach them:

A. *Assessment, like family development, is an ongoing process. Family goals, needs, and resources will change over time, and families will share more with you as trust develops.*

B. *Focus on the family's strengths, current situation, and future goals. When you help families evaluate their past experiences and influences, focus on how these affect their current situation and future goals.*

C. *Effective assessment is family-driven, not agency-centered. The primary goal of assessment is to help families become healthier and more self-reliant. While agencies do need to collect information about their own effectiveness, this requirement must not become more important than helping families assess their own needs.*

D. *Assessment with families is much more effective than assessment of or for families. Write down information with families, in plain language, and make sure they have a copy.*

E. *Collect only the information you need, and treat it with great care. Ask the family's permission to share their information with someone else. When you ask, be specific about what you're sharing, whom you're sharing it with, and why you're sharing it. Also, have the family member sign a release form before sharing their information.*

F. *Assessment must be respectful and culturally appropriate to the family you're working with.*

G. *There are sometimes good reasons to use standardized assessment, such as for collaborative agreements between agencies to make it easy for families to get services, or for research/program planning to improve services. Yet often families benefit more from an individualized assessment.*

Too often agency forms and procedures work against the strengths-based family development process. Many of these forms and assessment procedures are more appropriate to the deficit-oriented service provision model than to the family development approach. Some forms and procedures may be outdated but still in use because no one has reviewed them since the agency decided to use a family development approach, or because a state or federal funder requires the agency to use them.

A good way to start the process of evaluating ongoing assessments is by gathering all the standardized forms used by family workers, supervisors, and non-frontline agency staff. These forms might include, but are not limited to, intake and eligibility forms, individual service or family plans, progress notes, employment applications, performance reviews, or interim program and annual agency reports.

Even if your agency has report forms that funders require, you can still review the forms for ways to provide more comprehensive information on empowerment-based goals and outcomes. Whether the assessment forms you use are for internal agency purposes only, or are shared with collaborators and funders, these criteria can help you determine their effectiveness as empowerment-based assessment tools:

- *Empowerment-based assessment is process-oriented.* Most agencies, even those unfamiliar with using a family development approach, use ongoing assessment as a basic means of verifying a family's demographic information. When families must complete the same intake form every time they come to a different department in the agency—and perhaps even multiple times for different services— assessment becomes content-oriented. In contrast, *process-oriented assessment* is based on the recognition that each family's goals, needs, and resources *will* change over time.

  Process-oriented assessment is also useful in assessing a worker's goals, needs, and resources over time. Assessing a worker's performance using the same rating categories every year is counterproductive to building a worker's competencies through personalized goal setting and feedback.

- *Empowerment-based assessment is flexible.* Conventional standardized assessments typically emphasize broad-based outcomes and goals with little or no acknowledgement of the multiple secondary goals achieved in the process. Annual program review forms that measure the success of a program solely on the number of families that achieved their final goal miss unique opportunities to report achievement of unanticipated and secondary goals.

  Empowerment-based assessment reflects a core family development principle that "families must choose their own goals and methods of achieving them." Agencies do need assessment methods that encourage families to make progress, so that valuable agency resources are not monopolized by families who lack the motivation necessary for the family development process. But assessment tools and procedures must be flexible enough to consider a family's changing goals and circumstances.

Families should not be labeled as failures if they take a detour from the goal they set initially. Many agencies rely too heavily on information provided at the first meeting. Agencies using a family development approach recognize that as families grow to trust workers, they usually share more information over time.

- *Empowerment-based assessment focuses on strengths.* Most assessment methods focus on problems rather than on strengths. While there are important reasons to accurately assess risk and problems, these methods of assessment are generally most useful in crisis situations.

  Empowerment-based assessment forms should provide space for both the family worker and the family to note the family's strengths. Family workers often say that, initially, families find it very difficult to talk or write about their own strengths. However, given time and gentle encouragement, families usually begin to respond enthusiastically to this process. Assessment forms used for hiring new staff members, completing performance reviews, and reporting on the status and outcomes of interagency collaborations should provide enough space for everyone involved to reflect on the strengths of individual workers and partners.

In *Empowerment Skills for Family Workers*, the Family Development Plan is recommended as a simple assessment tool based on the seven basic principles of empowerment-based assessment identified earlier. Increasingly, agencies are replacing their old forms with the Family Development Plan, which is designed to help family workers focus their attention on the outcome of a family development relationship. A copy of the Family Development Plan is included in the Appendix.

Assessments such as the Family Development Plan incorporate both standardized and individualized assessment forms as part of an ongoing relationship between family and worker. Front-line supervisors can offer invaluable insights on the effectiveness of current ongoing assessment forms because they gather and compile large amounts of information from frontline workers that they synthesize for reports.

When workers first begin to use empowerment-based assessment tools, there can be a wide variety of reactions. Some, seeing the limitations of conventional assessment forms and methods, are eager to try new approaches. Others become anxious and resistant, and see this change as simply having to complete yet another form (when, in fact, doing so often means fewer forms in the long run.)

When questions are left blank or are unanswered on a standardized form, workers are prompted by the blank space to follow up for a response. Standardized assessments leave little room for interpretation. Yet workers may initially feel that individualized forms leave too much room for interpretation and require a level of professional judgment that they find uncomfortable.

Here are some helpful things for supervisors and agency leaders to know about the ways in which a shift to empowerment-based assessment will affect their organization:

- While leaders need to be clear about time frames and expectations for completing assessments, they also need to express trust in workers' abilities to schedule and make efficient use of their time. Especially during an agency's early transition to using new tools, workers greatly benefit from regular reassurance and helpful, nonjudgmental feedback.

- Leaders must commit to helping families learn and practice skills, and to providing workers with the time to listen, teach skills, and follow up with families. Empowerment-based assessment takes time for workers and families to get to know each other and develop mutual respect.

- *Supervisors and leaders must review and revise forms and procedures that cling to a deficit-oriented approach.* Agency leaders need to make changes in outdated, deficit-based forms. Workers and families are justified in feeling disgruntled, or even betrayed, when empowerment-based assessment is misinterpreted by leaders as adding a few more forms to the existing ones. Families can read between the lines when a helping organization "talks the talk" about an empowerment approach but "walks the walk" from a deficit one.

- Family workers may be resistant to empowerment-based assessment because it requires greater personal judgment and leaves more room for interpretation. Supporting workers by providing training and strengths-based feedback about ways to prepare new forms reduces the underlying anxiety that's often the underlying reason behind their resistance.

There are three ways to consider designing or revising your agency's ongoing assessment forms. The first is to review the forms currently used by the agency to determine if they reflect the principles of empowerment-based assessment outlined earlier in this chapter. Second, you can ask a service partner or other agency in your network who you feel is already using strength-based assessments if you can review blank copies of their forms.

A third way is to design a form assessing a new program or initiative. For example, consider creating an agency "Family's Bill of Rights," a family-worker confidentiality statement, and a professional development plan for staff members to use in conjunction with annual performance reviews. You may want to ask your staff members and colleagues to form a committee to design or revise assessment forms. The committee could even include several family members served by your agency, as well as workers from other agencies with whom you collaborate.

Connecting with state and national family support initiatives

Connecting with state and national coalitions and associations is a great way to support your own development, as well as to gain access to resources that can be shared with staff. It's also a way to expand your professional support network. Here are just a couple examples:

New York State Parenting Education Partnership (NYSPEP)

In 2006, a team representing public and private New York state agencies came together to consider how to increase a family's ability to nurture positive development in their children. They convened a statewide forum for a diverse group of parenting education providers, and the NYSPEP was launched.

The Coalition established a Parenting Education Credential, which defines consistent criteria and core competencies needed by all parenting educators to provide quality parent education programs. In New York, some of those applying for this credential have used FDC training to meet part of the requirement. They also provide professional development through regional training opportunities, a summer institute, and webinars.

Another component of NYSPEP is promoting "Community Cafes" throughout the state. Community Cafes are a tool to build communities capacity for action that strengthens families. Parent leaders facilitate conversations on topics identified as community needs, which leads to developing action steps that utilize existing community resources, support parent leadership, and promote healthy child development. NYSPEP provides training and support to staff from nonprofits who facilitate the Community Cafe process in their local communities. Their website is www.nyspep.org.

National Association for Family, School and Community Engagement (NAFSCE)

The National Association for Family, School and Community Engagement is an association focused on advancing high impact policies and practices for family, school, and community engagement to promote child development and improve student achievement. They offer several different professional learning opportunities, including webinars featuring national experts, and Member Connect, an online community comprised of groups of family engagement professionals who meet regularly, share expertise, and work collaboratively to improve and advance family engagement strategies.

They also convene an annual conference and have an extensive online library containing the latest research, articles, toolkits, and websites to help you develop programs and enhance your knowledge of best practices. Twice monthly newsletters relay the latest research in family development, describe innovative programs and policy developments, and more. Both individual and organizational membership is available. Their website is www.nafsce.org.

---

[10] L. Shulman, *Interactional Supervision* (Washington, DC: NASW Press, 1993).

[11] C. Glickman, S. Gordon, and J. Ross-Gordon, *SuperVision and Instructional leadership: A Developmental Approach* (Needham Heights, MA: Allyn & Bacon, 2001).

[12] Sara Horton-Deutsch, "Thinking It Through: The Path to Reflective Leadership, *American Nurse Today* 8, no. 2 (2013). http://americannursetoday.com/thinking-it-through-the-path-to-reflective-leadership/.

[13] Rebecca Parlakian and Nancy L. Seibel, "Being in Charge: Reflective Leadership in Infant and Family Programs" (Washington, DC: Zero to Three, 2001).

[14] Elizabeth Allworth, "Reflective Leadership: How Reflection Leads to Improved Performance" (August 2017). http://linkedin.com/pulse/reflective-leadership-how-reflection-leads-improved-allworth.

[15] G. L. Taggart and A. P. Wilson, *Promoting Reflective Thinking in Teachers*, 2nd ed. (Thousand Oaks, CA: Calvin Press, 2005).

[16] Süleyman Davut Göker and Kıvanç Bozkuş, "Reflective Leadership, Learning to Manage and Lead Human Organizations, Contemporary Leadership Challenges," in *Contemporary Leadership Challenges*, edited by Aida Alvinius (IntechOpen.com, February 2017), https://doi.org/10.5772/64968.

[17] D. Frick and L. Spears, eds., *On Becoming a Servant Leader: The Private Writings of Robert K. Greenleaf* (San Francisco: Jossey-Bass, 1996).

[18] J. Lipman-Blumen, *The Connective Edge: Leading in an Interdependent World* (San Francisco: Jossey-Bass, 1996).

[19] Ibid.

[20] Daniel Goleman, *Working with Emotional Intelligence* (New York: Bantam, 2000).

[21] L. Ackerman and D. Anderson, *The Change Leader's Roadmap: How to Navigate Your Organization's Transformation* (San Francisco: Jossey-Bass/Pfeiffer, 2001).

Chapter 2—Additional Resources

Books

Ackerman Anderson, L., and D. Anderson. *The Change Leader's Roadmap: How to Navigate Your Organization's Transformation.* San Francisco: Jossey-Bass, 2001.

Bennis, W., and J. Goldsmith. *Learning to Lead: A Workbook on Becoming a Leader.* Boston: Perseus, 1997.

Blanchard, K., J. Carlos, and A. Randolph. *Empowerment Takes More than a Minute.* New York: MFJ, 1996.

Block, P. *The Empowered Manager: Positive Political Skills at Work.* San Francisco: Jossey-Bass, 1987.

Frick, D., and L. Spears, eds. *On Becoming a Servant Leader: The Private Writings of Robert K. Greenleaf.* San Francisco: Jossey-Bass, 1996.

Glickman, C., S. Gordon, and J. Ross-Gordon. *SuperVision and Instructional Leadership: A Developmental Approach.* Needham Heights, MA: Allyn & Bacon, 2001.

Goleman, Daniel. *Working with Emotional Intelligence.* New York: Bantam, 2000.

Lipman-Blumen, Jean. *The Connective Edge: Leading in an Interdependent World.* San Francisco: Jossey-Bass, 1996. (The Achieving Styles Situational Assessment Inventory [ASSAI] was developed by Jean Lipman-Blumen. For more information on the inventory, see www.achievingstyles.com.)

Price-Waterhouse Change Integration Team. *Best Practices for Transforming Your Organization.* New York: McGraw-Hill, 1995.

Rath, Tom. Strengths Finder 2.0. Gallup, 2007.

Shulman, L. *Interactional Supervision.* Washington: NASW, 1993.

Articles

Dale Carnegie & Associates. "Recognizing leadership blind spots and discovering the road to motivating your employees." 2017. https://www.adhq.com/uploads/stories/story-file-WHite-Paper-LeadershipBlindspotwp050817-.

Economy, P. "7 Secrets of Servant Leadership that Will Lead You to Success." *Inc.* 2015. https://www.inc.com/peter-economy/7-secrets-of-servant-leadership-that-will-lead-you-to-success.html.

Hendricks, D. "6 Ways to Empower Your Employees with Transformational Leadership." *Forbes* (2014). https://forbes.com/sites/drewhendricks/2014/01/27/6-ways-to-empower-your-employees-with-transformational-leadership/#2657c8361ada.

Lipman-Blumen, J. "Connective Leadership: Our Last Great Leadership Hope. *New York Times,* March 8, 2013.

Plett, Heather. "What It Really Means to 'Hold Space' for People, Plus Eight Tips on How to Do It Well." Blogpost, 11 March 2015. https://heatherplett.com/2015/03/hold-space/.

Spears, L. C. "Character and Servant Leadership: Ten Characteristics of Effective, Caring Leaders." *Journal of Virtues and Leadership* 1 (2010): 25-30.

Süleyman, Davut Göker, and Kivanç Bozkuş. "Reflective Leadership: Learning to Manage and Lead Human Organizations. In *Contemporary Leadership Challenges,* edited by Alda Alvinius, 27-45. IntechOpen.com, 2017. https://doi.org/10.5772/64968.

Worksheet

The Leadership Compass Self-Assessment. Be the Change Consulting, 2010.

Website

Clifton Strengths Assessment. Strengths Finder. http://www.gallupstrengthscenter.com/.

Ideas for Independent Learning Projects

The following are suggestions for independent learning projects to increase your knowledge in transforming your workplace through empowerment-based leadership. *We encourage you to develop your own independent learning project that is relevant to your workplace, or make modifications to the ones listed below to create a meaningful and manageable plan.*

- Learn more about level of empowerment in your workplace using the *Empowerment Skills for Leaders* Sentence Completion Sheet at the end of this chapter. Make three copies of the sheet. On one sheet, write your responses following the directions. Invite two people you know well but who have different relationships to family support work (e.g., family worker, interagency colleague, co-leader, or family member) to complete a form. Review the three completed forms, and write a reflection on the similarities and differences you found on how you and others feel about family support and self-empowerment.

- Review your agency's standardized forms in one of the following areas: family intake and goal-setting, employment application packet, performance reviews, or monthly program reporting. Using the FDC principles for empowerment-based assessment presented in this chapter, identify ways that the forms promote or hinder support for families and staff. Share your findings with your supervisor or a co-leader and ask for feedback. Write a reflection that identifies ways that your organization can redesign or revise the forms to promote empowerment-based relationships.

- Contact a representative of a family support association in your area and inquire about their current initiatives. Ask about their accomplishments and challenges in promoting the principles of family support. Write a reflection on what you learn, and identify ways you can support these efforts in your agency and community.

- Using the Workplace Empowerment Plan from the chapter, select a goal for workplace empowerment within your organization. Write a reflection on the process and any initial progress.

Empowerment Skills for Leaders Sentence Completion Sheet

First Name: _____

Please write your first response after reading each of the following sentence fragments.

1. People have difficulties in their lives because _____

_____

2. The most important thing you need in life is _____

_____

3. The main reason families come to helping organizations is _____

_____

4. The most important thing families need to become healthy and self-reliant is _____

_____

5. Families experience problems and crises on an ongoing basis because _____

_____

Thank you for your participation.

Chapter 3
Leadership and Self-Empowerment

Learning objectives

- Develop or clarify a personal leadership vision for your work.
- Practice listening and communication skills that focus on "being present."
- Understand the qualities of mindful leadership.
- Practice simple strategies for incorporating mindfulness in daily activities.
- Assess the types of supports and stressors you experience in the workplace.
- Create a good balance between your work and personal life.
- Develop and practice steps in a personal stress reduction and wellness program.

Clarifying a personal vision for your work

Effective leaders are both visionary and practical. They hold a clear and evolving vision—and they take good care of themselves. Have there been times when you've changed your job, put educational plans on hold, reduced your work hours to care for a young child or sick loved one, or relocated to another place to express your inner beliefs or stay connected to a person? Developing a personal vision is like making a commitment to an inner belief or to another person, except that you're making the commitment to yourself.

A personal vision is not as much a description of what you are *doing* as a leader, but rather an expression of your true *being*. When you develop a clear personal vision for your work, you realize that each person you work with and each job you hold can support and shape that vision.

A supervisor who participated in an FDC Leadership Initiative focus group said:

> So often workers and staff are told to do something, but they don't know the purpose behind it. I think that sharing that vision with them and being very clear about why you're doing something and the rationale behind it, is really important.

> Once in a workshop we were asked to describe the qualities of a good employee. Then, we were asked to describe a good supervisor. Things we listed like honesty, integrity, and communication skills were identified in both.

Some people already have a clear vision of exactly the kind of work they want to do. Often, this clarity comes from personal experience. Whether you're new to your role as a leader in your organization or have held the same job for years, it's never too late to develop or update a personal vision for your work. It's also important to revisit your vision periodically to stay connected to the most important person capable of making that vision a reality—*you*.

What if your vision isn't quite clear or has become clouded over time? Take a few minutes, now or at some other more convenient time, to step back from your work and ask yourself these questions:

- Why did I go into this kind of work?
- Are these reasons still important to me?
- What is really important in my life?
- What special talents do I have to offer?
- Is there something I'd rather be doing? If so, how can I move in that direction?

Shifting your focus from "doing" to "being"

How do you feel when you're with someone who gives you their undivided attention? Imagine how that would feel—no cell phones, no interruptions, just you and the other person listening to one another. This quality of presence, being totally awake and aware at each moment, is the essence of empowering leadership. Although few people can sustain this quality of presence for long periods of time, you can begin today to cultivate your unique capacity to be more fully present with others.

But first, you'll need to practice being present with yourself. Do you arrive at your office breathless, your mind already racing through a long list of "to-dos"? There's nothing wrong with having a to-do list, but if you want to live more fully, try shifting your focus from getting things done to being more present with each person you encounter and everything you do. Don't worry, you'll still be able to cross those tasks off your to-do list, but you'll do so with deeper understanding and creativity.

Developing a clear mind

Leading others requires a clear mind. How can we develop a clear mind amidst the ever-shifting challenges of leading? Your *brain* contains billions of intricately interconnected firing neurons directing every part of your body and mind. Growing evidence shows that *mind* goes far beyond the physical workings of your brain. Among the many definitions of mind, one that is most appropriate to our work has been put forth by Dr. Daniel Siegel, a professor of psychiatry at UCLA School of Medicine in his book *Mind: A Journey to the Heart of being Human.*[22] Dr. Siegel describes *mind* as "the emergent self-organizing process, both embodied and relational, that regulates energy and information flow within and among us."

So, how does a clear mind help us to lead? And how can we develop a clear mind? An uncluttered mind promotes *cognitive flexibility*, the ability to sort through and initiate appropriate responses (or refrain from acting) to the multitude of global, national, local, environmental, humanitarian, political, financial, personal, and work issues we're faced with daily. Thus, before leading anyone else, leaders must first manage their own emotions and practical matters.

You can take specific actions to build a stronger brain, which in turn contributes to developing a clear mind. Recent developments in brain science show that the brain's neuroplasticity is constantly reinventing itself. There's much we can do to promote brain health, especially through exercise, eating healthily, and maintaining healthy relationships. In this chapter, we suggest strategies for all these approaches. In the words of Daniel Goleman:

> *The emotional brain responds to an event more quickly than the thinking brain. Mindful meditation has been discovered to foster the ability to inhibit those very quick emotional impulses.*

Mindful leadership

This quality of being and awareness is called *mindfulness*. It's a *moment-to-moment awareness of what is*. In the study of creativity, mindfulness is sometimes called "flow." In athletics, it's sometimes called "being in the zone." Mindfulness is not something you have to acquire—you already have it. It's your natural birthright. As a baby, you played, delighted in every aspect of each moment: the experience of dust specks in the sunshine or cooking aromas, cuddling with loving parents or caregivers. But by the time you reached adulthood, millions of messages blunted that keen awareness and natural intuitive intelligence you'd had as a baby. Mindfulness is a practice to recover some of your natural capacity to be joyfully and fully present in your life.

Why is mindfulness especially important for leaders? In *Finding the Space to Lead*, Janice Marturano states:

> *Scientific research has shown that mindfulness practices enhance mental health and improve performance in every field of endeavor. And leaders who have undergone mindfulness training report that it provides a 'transformative experience' that significantly improves their innovation, self-awareness, listening and decision-making.*

In her books *Mindfulness* and *The Power of Mindful Learning*,[23] Ellen Langer suggests using mindfulness as an approach to counteract the inclination to think and act in "mindless" and unconscious ways. For example, read the following message that typically appears at the close of most professional correspondence:

Thank you for your time and and attention with this matter.

Just the typical closing sentence to a letter? If you noticed the extra "and" in the middle of the sentence, you were probably reading with a more alert, mindful approach than most people normally bring to daily life. Mindfulness brings increased awareness to everything and everyone you encounter. This awareness can bring situations to your attention while they're still in the early stages, when it's easier to redirect them, if necessary. *Intuition*—your subtle inner wisdom—thrives in a mindful atmosphere.

As a leader and supervisor, you have so much to do every day. You might be thinking that, even if it were possible to give undivided attention to every task and person, you could never get everything done. However, being mindful is *not* just another management technique; it's an approach to leadership that allows you to:

- Appreciate the creative ways that consulting with others can expand your perspective and capacity to find new and innovative solutions
- Bring all of "who you are" as a unique individual to the experience of being a leader
- Realign your leadership style with your leadership vision for empowering yourself and others
- Reframe the outdated and limiting view of leadership based on "command and control" into one of leadership through empowerment and transformation
- Transform mindless conditioned responses into fresh, aware living

In her book *Finding the Space to Lead: A Practical Guide to Mindful Leadership*,[24] Janice Marturano describes her own pathway to mindful leadership. She notes the many challenges leaders face today that reinforce why cultivating mindful practice is so important. These include the complex economic and resource constraints facing many organizations, and a mobile workforce seeking better opportunities that contribute to frequent turnover of staff. We're also attached 24/7 to an array of technological devices that can be anxiety-producing as well as helpful. The sheer volume of information at our disposal can be overwhelming, and the multitude of opinions on any given subject can be daunting, making it difficult to determine what's reliable.

While there are many qualities of an effective leader, Marturano lists two that are "must haves": the ability to connect to self, to others, and to the larger community; and the ability of a leader to skillfully guide change. She goes on to say that "skillfully" doesn't mean commanding or controlling, but rather collaborating and listening with an open mind. Going deeper into these two capacities, there are four fundamentals of leadership excellence that help to develop them: focus, clarity, creativity, and compassion—all of which can be strengthened through mindfulness practice.

Focus

Focus is our ability to pay attention and stay on task. In this technological world, it's hard not to be distracted by the sound of an email or text coming in. Over time, we're conditioned to check that message, just in case it's something important, and respond immediately. The latest social media posts also await our review. How often have you observed someone looking down at their phone during a meeting or training, or even done it yourself? Work-related messages may also come in during our time off, distracting us from family time or leisure activities. Another factor is the sheer volume of work we need to accomplish daily, pushing our thoughts ahead to the next item on our to-do list.

The result of all these distractions is loss of productivity. At work, it could mean taking longer to finish a grant proposal, or leaving a meeting while feeling unsure of what was decided on. It can also lead to a loss of connectivity with others who might feel you're not fully listening as your body language indicates your thoughts are jumping ahead to the next meeting. Strengthening focus takes practice, but you can learn to notice when your mind wanders away from the present moment, as well as how to redirect it back to the present.

Clarity

Clarity is the ability to clearly see issues and opportunities, and to *choose* how to respond. This might mean challenging our own assumptions. As Marturano suggests, sometimes this clarity helps us decide that the right response to a situation is to do nothing at all, and wait and see what develops—despite our inclination to take some action. It calls for strengthening our ability to see not only events and the environment around us, but also to see ourselves more clearly. Noticing how we react to certain situations, and the ways our conditioning and experiences may be filtering out some of what we need to see, can lead us to make important changes. This process of self-reflection and self-examination helps leaders to work skillfully with their colleagues and staff to effect change.

Creativity

Creativity allows us to think out of the box and come up with innovative solutions and ideas. Recent brain science teaches us that creativity requires some slow time for the brain.[25] However, with our calendars filled with meetings and tasks to accomplish, our brains seldom get the space needed for creativity. Constantly focusing on tasks gets in the way of the "wisdom that lies deep within us,"[26] according to Marturano. That explains why ideas often pop into our heads when we least expect them, such as when we're taking a walk in the park or soaking in a bath. Practicing mindfulness can help us allow more space for developing creative solutions to issues in the workplace.

Compassion

Compassion helps us to better understand ourselves and others, and to recognize the commonalities we all share. In the *Empowerment Skills for Workers* course, we talk about empathy and the importance of trying to "put yourself in another's shoes." Compassion is an even stronger feeling of understanding and wanting to lessen the suffering or misfortune of others. Part of developing our ability for compassion is realizing that sometimes we may create suffering—for others and for ourselves.

Self-compassion is thus also essential and often very difficult to achieve. Those of us in the human-services field tend to place the needs of everyone else above our own. Not to do so might even feel selfish or self-indulgent.

But having compassion for ourselves and taking care of our own needs helps us to open our hearts more fully to allow the space for compassion for others. Taking care of ourselves also prevents burnout and the resentment that sometimes builds up when life seems overwhelming.

The best leaders model self-care and compassion for others. In this chapter, we offer strategies for self-care and exercises to help you develop mindful leadership and the space to lead.

Mindfulness-based stress reduction

As a leader you encounter the same stressors as those you supervise, compounded by responsibilities for funding, government regulation, interagency collaboration, personnel issues, and interactions with your supervisor, board, or committees. You need a stress reduction program that really works. *Empowerment Skills for Family Workers* gives front-line workers practical, effective stress-management techniques. This topic has been one of the most impactful for those who take the course. For some, it has been life changing. Initially, National FDC Director Claire Forest was pleased that workers were learning such useful stress management skills, but a further analysis of the FDC portfolios made her realize how inherently stressful front-line family work really is. She asked herself, "Is something more than stress *management* needed? If so, who in the United States is doing the most effective work in this area?"

Claire found that the University of Massachusetts Medical Center's Stress Reduction Clinic had the most impressive record in settings similar to those in which human service professionals work. At the time, the clinic already had twenty-five years of research from its work in free community clinics, public schools, and workplaces. Using the "mindfulness-based stress reduction" methods developed at the University of Massachusetts, men and women from a range of cultural backgrounds and life circumstances experienced significant reductions in serious stress-related illnesses.

Intrigued by these impressive results, Claire spent a week taking the professional training offered by the Stress Reduction Clinic's founder, Dr. Jon Kabat-Zinn, and its director, Dr. Saki Santorelli. There, she learned to bring moment-to-moment awareness—mindfulness—to everyday activities such as breathing, walking, sitting, and eating. She tried the "body scan" technique developed at the Clinic—bringing gentle awareness to each part of the body—and practiced simple stretching exercises. She felt knots of stress unwind in ways that twenty years of practicing and teaching "stress management" had not touched. Perhaps best of all, practicing mindfulness-based stress reduction doesn't cost anything; nor does it require any special gear.

Kabat-Zinn and Santorelli emphasize that before teaching mindfulness-based stress reduction to others, a person should practice it daily for at least one year. They recommend at least 45 minutes of practice daily. Claire followed their recommendations, and one year later incorporated these practices into FDC training and its curriculum. Since that time, FDC participants, in their Overall Course Reflections, overwhelmingly describe how impactful and transformative the chapters on Presence and Mindfulness and Taking Care of Self have been in their lives, both personally and professionally.

There are many excellent resources on mindfulness-based practice listed at the end of this chapter, including books by Kabat-Zinn. As an introduction to practicing mindfulness-based stress reduction, here are some simple exercises to start with.

Mindfulness practice exercises

Mindful breathing

Perhaps you're ready to try mindfulness practice but wonder how to begin. You won't need any special equipment; just find a quiet spot with a comfortable chair. Start with 10 minutes of mindful breathing.

1. To begin, you can close your eyes (although it's okay keep your eyes open, if you prefer) and bring your awareness to the sounds around you: birds, traffic, people talking, whatever noises you hear.

2. As you settle in, you'll become aware of more subtle sounds, such the air conditioning or heating. Let go of those noises, and pay attention to your breathing coming in, then going out.

3. Concentrate on your breathing and experience the sensations of your body as you inhale and exhale.

4. If thoughts begin to arise during this exercise, gently bring your attention back to your breathing.

5. Feel any emotions that arise, but don't let the story behind the emotion occupy your attention.

6. After a few minutes and when you are ready, open your eyes, and slowly bring yourself back to your external world.

Mindful breathing will help you feel refreshed, peaceful, and ready to meet whatever the next part of your day brings.

Mindful walking

If you're basically comfortable with the mindfulness breathing practice but get bored or too distracted, try mindful walking. Usually, we gallop from place to place, barely noticing how we got there. Mindful walking invites you to pay special attention to the usually unconscious activity of walking.

1. Lift one foot gently, slowly, off the ground.

2. Pay attention to each muscle as your foot leaves the ground.

3. Be aware of the miraculous coordination of bones, muscles, and sinews that work with your brain to enable you to lift your foot.

4. Notice where your body weight is resting.

5. When you're ready, slowly place that foot onto the ground.

6. Feel yourself fully grounded before gradually shifting your weight.

7. Keep breathing.

8. When you're ready, mindfully lift your other foot.

Try walking in this way for three minutes, bringing your full moment-to-moment awareness to the process. You will cover very little ground. The purpose is not to get somewhere, but to be fully present where you are. Try bringing this same quality of attention to other things you do routinely, such as responding to a text. Instead of immediately looking at the message, you could let it be a signal to be mindful *before* you read it and respond.

Mindful stretching

Do you spend much of your day sitting in meetings, at the computer, or in a car? Try mindful stretching. Just getting up out of your chair can restore your mindfulness.

1. Start by standing up and stretching your arms overhead, and then let them fall back to your sides.
2. Gently roll your shoulders forward and then back.

A little mindful stretching can do wonders to relax and bring awareness to your body. Better yet, take a class in stretching or yoga, or find an exercise coach to come to your workplace to provide gentle stretching classes.

Mindful listening

Leaders spend hours each day listening. Chapter 4, Supervising with Skill and Heart, offers practice in using advanced-level communication skills to help you say what you mean—carefully, clearly, and respectfully. Listening affords an ideal way to practice mindfulness. Instead of speaking and then focusing on your reply, bring your full attention to listening to the other person. Every encounter is an opportunity to practice mindfully listening to another. This is similar to mindful walking. Imagine that you've never listened to anyone before, then bring that fresh, curious perspective to the other person.

Mindful living

Mindfulness isn't just a skill to learn—it's an approach to life. No one ever lives mindfully in every moment. However, mindfulness deepens with time and practice. It can help you live life to its fullest, and bring forth your natural compassion and intuitive intelligence.

Practical strategies for mindful leadership

"Can I be mindful and still get things done?"

Although increasing your level of awareness can enhance every area of your life, you'll find it especially helpful in your work as a leader or supervisor. When you first consider adding mindfulness practice to your day, it's natural to worry about how you can fit in yet another activity without neglecting your responsibilities. Working mindfully doesn't mean that you throw away your to-do list; it means that you strive to bring your full awareness to *all* of your activities.

By working mindfully, you'll save the time needed to reorient yourself to your task when you get called away or take a break; you'll still be aware of where you were. As you become increasingly mindful, you'll naturally feel more inclined to eliminate distractions that can take energy away from your real work. You'll have fewer time-consuming mistakes to correct. And, as you bring more mindfulness to interactions with staff members, they'll begin to work more harmoniously and efficiently as well. If you choose to become a more mindful leader, you'll still do most of the same things you did before, but you'll approach your work in a profoundly different way.

Spending your time on what is important

Look at your calendar. Are there things on your schedule that you don't want to do and don't really have to do? If so, cancel them right now. Don't be apologetic, just be polite and firm. You might say, "I have been happy to serve on the _____ committee for the past eight years, but it's time for me to resign now because of other commitments. Please send my best to the others. It was a pleasure to work with you." Then put something in that time slot on your calendar that will nourish you and your vision, such as an exercise class, a regular fun outing with friends or family, a time for mindfulness practice, a class at a college, or a walk in the park. Write these in on all your calendars. This will help you notice significant discrepancies between what activities you do and what it is that you really want to do.

Developing a daily to-do list will also help you prioritize and review your accomplishments at the end of each day. After you prepare your list, take a minute to step back, review it, and ask these questions:

- What tasks must be accomplished today?
- Are there so many things on my list that it will require "superhuman" stamina to do them all today?

Here are some tips to help you use your time effectively:

1. *Set realistic goals for your work and personal life.* As a leader, you're probably a "can do" person who routinely performs well under pressure and tight deadlines. Whenever you can, set timelines to finish a task, so you don't end up frantically rushing out the door late for a meeting, or to make a presentation.

2. *Listen to your intuition.* If you have a sense that you should connect with a collaborator, colleague, or worker about something, go ahead and do it. Successful collaborations start with relationship building, which takes time and personal connection.

3. *Focus your best energy on what is most important.* What time of day do you feel clearest and most productive? Try to schedule your most important work at that time. Concentrate on those tasks directly related to your work as a leader. Be careful about inadvertently taking on tasks that are the responsibility of others. Learning to delegate tasks to your employees not only develops important skills and shows trust, it also alleviates some of your own stress of having to get things done.

4. *Handle routine tasks efficiently.* Use technology wisely to save time. Try not to constantly check your email and text messages, and cut back on the time you spend on social media.

5. *Take time to learn how to use new office equipment and software programs.* Although doing so does take time initially, it will allow you to be more productive and efficient in the long run.

6. *"Never touch a paper twice" is a helpful motto to adopt in tackling paperwork and junk mail.* Arrange to have your name removed from lists you don't want to receive. When you receive correspondence that asks for a reply, consider making a quick phone call instead of composing a time-consuming, written response.

7. *Communicate efficiently.* Whenever you hear or receive program information, ask yourself: Who else needs to know this? Write down the information and names of people you need to share it with.

"It won't work for me—I don't have a door to close!"

Not everyone has an office door to close or can let messages go for a little while. Some jobs offer little opportunity for quiet reflection. In many work settings, it takes great creativity to find time and space for this kind of mindfulness practice. Claire worked in a storefront family center in which all staff shared one office, as a home visitor driving to families' homes, and in a day-care center, in which every moment is public time. As a home visitor, she paused for a moment on the front stoop of a home to "catch her breath" before knocking. Driving between appointments, she pulled over for a few minutes to reflect and return to mindfulness before going on to the next family or meeting.

Try a "mindful minute"

If spending the first minutes of your workday in mindfulness practice is something you can't comfortably imagine right now, try practicing a "mindful minute" during your day between meetings or telephone calls. You can practice this technique almost anywhere. You may think that stopping for only a minute won't do much good, but taking time regularly—particularly on stressful days—can help you regain the balance you need to lead effectively. This is especially true if you regularly make time for longer stretches of mindfulness practice, for example, at home. Here's how to spend a mindful minute:

1. Find a comfortable sitting position. Allow your body to relax, drop your shoulders, and rest your arms and legs. Close your eyes, or if you prefer, keep them open and focus on a comforting or neutral focal point in your workspace.

2. Start by listening to the subtle sounds around you, such as air moving or voices in the background. After a while, start to notice the sound of your own breathing, in and out.

3. As you notice your breath entering and leaving your body, if thoughts or emotions arise, merely notice them—don't follow their story line. Visualize them as clouds drifting by on a summer day. Bring your awareness to your body: the sensations of breathing in your chest and the beating of your heart. Become aware of and release any tension in your shoulders or arms. Notice how your back rests into the curve of the chair. Remain in that awareness for a few more moments. Notice how it feels to be relaxed and aware of your being in the world.

4. Then, gently make the transition back to your day at work. Listen for the sounds of the outside world coming back into focus. When you feel ready, open your eyes; sharpen your focus and attention on the objects you see at eye level. Then, after taking a deep breath, go back to your work or routine, and notice the effect that your mindful minute has on your energy, patience, and creativity.

Removing distractions

Our lives are filled with mindless distractions that rob us of our energy and keep us from focusing on what really matters. Here are some examples of distractions:

- TV, radio, and cell phones
- Text messages
- Social media
- Chatty co-workers
- Junk food
- Junk mail
- Shopping websites

For one day, keep a list of all the distractions in your life. Then choose one and do something to reduce its negative impact on your mindfulness. For example, look at your email. Does it include items you don't want to receive and end up deleting? Is it distracting you from more meaningful tasks? If so, unsubscribe from those email lists.

Do you use social media or turn on the news as soon as you wake up? Leave the TV off or put your cell phone down for a morning and focus on listening to your family members, or fully tasting your breakfast. If you live with others, you may need to make this a family experiment.

Probably technology has filled your life with new and rapidly multiplying forms of distraction. Anyone with a cell phone or tablet can, with a few quick key strokes, send you messages that are equally likely to contain drivel as useful information. Either way, they take your valuable time and attention.

How do you know when you've lost your mindfulness? If someone asks you, "How do you stand it when…?" and you reply, "I don't even notice it anymore", you may be so enmeshed in that particular distraction that you are no longer aware of its debilitating effect on your capacity to be present and mindful. These effects may have bypassed your mind, going straight into your body's ill health, or into maintaining addictions such as alcohol, cigarettes, food, drugs, sex, or gambling to numb the pain that comes from not living life fully.

Feeling good about the work you do

Healthy ways to express your feelings

Expressing your feelings respectfully and clearly is an essential skill for leaders. And you also need to skillfully handle feelings expressed by others. Today's collaborative workplaces require leaders to seek out and listen to others' insights. Even when you don't ask, someone will usually volunteer an opinion or express an emotion.

Your own thoughts and feelings can arise without notice. In a typical day, you may encounter situations that cause you to feel angry, sad, upset, happy, worried, or frightened. You'll need to make a conscious choice about whether to express those feelings.

Children usually have a more difficult time separating thoughts from feelings. For example, when they hear that a joyously anticipated event has been postponed, they often have an immediate and strong emotional response of disappointment, or even protest. They forget, in the heat of the moment, that they can choose how to react. Adults have a broader base of experience to inform their choices on the timing and intensity of their emotional reactions. They also know that their expression of feelings carries consequences for themselves and others. As a leader, finding healthy ways to express your feelings is an essential skill, especially when you're being blamed or criticized.

Conflict exists at all stages of life, both at work and at home. Although many people try to avoid conflict, disagreement can be productive. Skillfully managing small conflicts can prevent big problems from erupting. Disagreement can help people understand and become more open to others' points of view. Thoughtful confrontation can lead to needed change. It can be tempting to deny that a conflict exists by avoiding it, giving in, or attempting to impose instant solutions. None of these approaches works as well as collaborative problem-solving. In Chapter 4, Supervising with Skill and Heart, you'll learn more about how to skillfully resolve conflict.

Handling blame or criticism is one of the hardest and most stressful parts of being a leader or supervisor. Whether the criticism comes from your staff, your supervisor, board member, or a colleague, it's hard to avoid reacting defensively, or becoming depressed or angry. Some people internalize criticism, seeing it as "all my fault," while others see it as a personal attack and attempt to retaliate. Communication techniques such as paraphrasing, "I" messages," and feedback can help you understand your reactions, and express your feelings responsibly and effectively.

These skills work best when built on a foundation of mindfulness and, if practiced regularly, can help you remain peaceful in the midst of conflict. As you practice being mindful each day, you'll be prepared to remain clear about what's actually happening and choose your response(s) more wisely.

Have some fun

> *We do not stop playing because we grow old: We grow old because we stop playing.*
>
> –Anonymous

When was the last time you remember laughing and just having fun? Hopefully, it wasn't too long ago! As an adult, you may feel that "play" and "work" are opposites and that playfulness is childish and immature. But having fun and taking healthy risks nurtures your creativity and provides significant health benefits as well.

In *Living Your Life Out Loud*,[27] Salli Rasberry and Padi Swelwyn offer these ideas for taking "mini-breaks" in your day:

- Keep a book of cartoons, short essays, or a paperback book of daily aspirations on hand. Sometimes, the shortest distance between two moods is humor.
- Take off your shoes and give yourself a foot massage.

- Put on some relaxing music, close your eyes, and have a bona fide daydream.
- Sketch something in your immediate surroundings. Really look closely and notice all the details in your environment, some of which you may never have noticed before.
- Write a poem or silly limerick. Remember, you don't have to show it to anyone, so let loose—the point is to have fun!

Optimism and hardiness

Think of people you might know who personify the qualities expressed in these aphorisms:

She's someone who can roll with the punches.

He's a person who won't cry over spilled milk.

The team went back to work realizing it was "water under the bridge."

People with optimistic attitudes tend to cope more effectively with stress. They're more likely to use solution-focused coping skills to resolve difficulties (see Chapter 4, Supervising with Skill and Heart). This personality attribute is referred to as *hardiness*—an emotional characteristic found in people who feel they have significant control over their lives. They see challenges not merely as obstacles, but as opportunities that encourage their creativity and personal growth. Studies have found that commitment to seeing a situation through and having confidence in one's ability to successfully complete a task with an appropriate level of challenge are essential to individual hardiness.

Compassion and care for yourself

Did you go into human services work because you felt compassion for and wanted to help others? Perhaps you soon learned that it was not that simple. Maybe you began to shut down some of your natural empathy in the face of agency regulations, professional guidelines, and the daily grind of witnessing poverty and inequity. In the process, you may have protected yourself but also have lost some of your initial compassion.

Mindfulness can help you restore your empathy and compassion for yourself and others. Let's start with you. Can you offer yourself the same level of compassion you offer to others? Can you be kind to yourself? As you try to balance the ideals of service with the realities of life, there will be tension between meeting your needs and those of other people. Accept the fact that it's impossible to be there for everybody all the time. Recognize that this isn't because you have shortcomings, but because life will always ask more of you than you could possibly give.

Try to develop compassion for yourself, realizing that you can't do everything, and that it's okay to fall short of your ideals. If you treat yourself with compassion and care, you'll have renewed energy to decide what's important and follow through.

Here is a recipe for taking good care of yourself:

- Recognize when stress becomes overstress.
- Practice mindfulness-based stress reduction.
- Share your feelings in healthy solution-focused ways.
- Incorporate some fun into your everyday schedule.

Appropriate Intimacy

Mindful relationships with staff, colleagues, and those you serve often feel very intimate. When you listen mindfully to someone, you offer a kind of intimacy that some people have seldom—or perhaps never—

experienced. As a leader, you have an opportunity to model such relationships. You can be genuine and honest in building caring relationships with others while safeguarding your privacy and theirs.

As a leader, you also have a special responsibility to establish appropriate boundaries because of the inherent power your position carries. That means finding the right balance between a genuinely friendly and caring relationship with staff as well as a supervisory one.

Creating a support system for yourself

In your role as leader, you provide support for your colleagues and staff. You deserve similar support in your own work. In *Empowerment Skills for Family Workers*, participants are introduced to the Family Circles Assessment to help reflect on how they're influenced by their immediate family, extended family, friends, neighbors, co-workers, community institutions, the culture, the economy, and the natural environment.[28] They complete this assessment themselves and, working with others in the training, practice skills in helping families use this tool to identify their supports, stressors, and strengths.

The following diagram is an adaptation of the Family Circles Assessment for you to use in identifying your own strengths, stressors, and supports. Although some of the categories and descriptions have been revised for leaders, this adaptation incorporates the same seven circles to list the people, institutions, and social trends that affect your healthy self-reliance and empowerment. Follow the directions on the next page to complete the assessment.

The Family Circles Assessment adapted for leaders

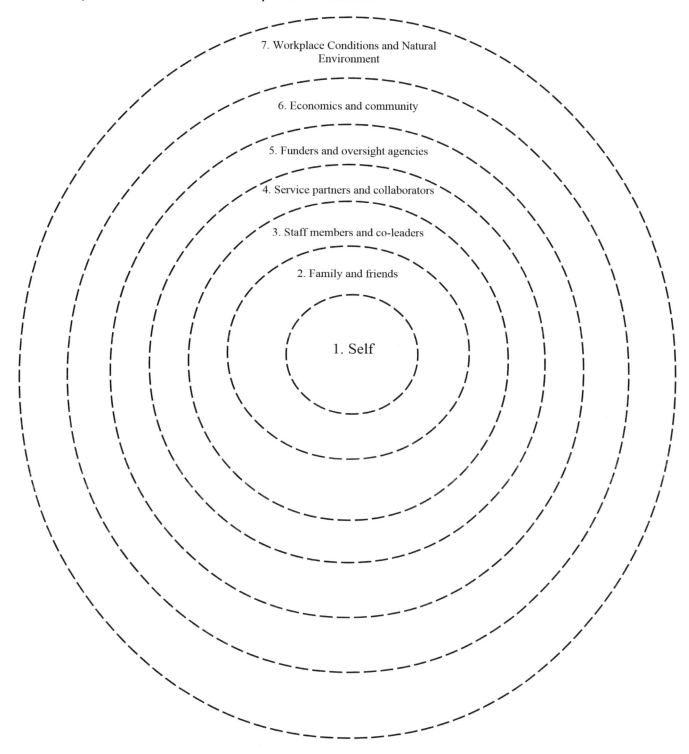

7. Workplace Conditions and Natural Environment

6. Economics and community

5. Funders and oversight agencies

4. Service partners and collaborators

3. Staff members and co-leaders

2. Family and friends

1. Self

Note: The lines between the circles are dotted to show they are fluid. You decide where to list someone.

Write your responses on the Circles sheet, using these guidelines:

1. *Yourself*: You are at the center of your world. List your guiding principles of leadership and personal vision for your work. Note your leadership strengths, dreams, and goals. Also note any qualities or conditions that influence your leadership.

2. *Family members and friends*: List names of your partner (if you have one), family members, and friends. Note their qualities, any relationship aspects that mean a lot to you, and how these relationships influence your leadership.

3. *Staff members, your supervisor, co-leaders, or board members*: List names of those who you communicate with at work on a daily basis. You might also include the names of individuals who you feel significantly contribute to you and your agency's overall well-being (e.g., professional colleagues, volunteers, community supporters, key advisors). Note the ways in which they influence you and your agency.

4. *Service partners and collaborators*: List the names of individuals or agencies that work with your agency in providing family support in your community. Note the ways in which they influence you or your agency. You can also identify your agency's professional associations, interagency networks, and state and national affiliations.

5. *Funders and oversight agencies*: List the primary funders for your program(s) or agency and, if different, the names of departments that oversee and monitor agency outcomes. Note the ways in which they influence you and your agency.

6. *Economics and community*: Note the social, political, and economic influences that currently affect your role and work as a leader (e.g., impact of agency/department reorganization, funding cuts, government regulations). Describe your community and how it affects your workplace. Note how local, state, national, and global trends affect you as a leader.

7. *Workplace conditions and natural environment*: Note how workplace conditions and the natural environment affect you in your agency (e.g., lack of privacy, ease/difficulty of commuting to work, travel required to programs at different locations, a nearby park for walks during lunch breaks, level of safety for workers on home visits).

Now that you've completed this leader adaptation of the Family Circles Assessment, do you have a good mental picture of the people and influences that shape your work life? Go back and look at this "map" of the influences in your life. Are your circles uniformly full of notations? If one of your circles is brimming over while another is nearly empty, this may be indicative of an imbalance in your work environment. For example, if the "service partners and collaborators" circle is full of items, but the one for "workplace conditions and natural environment" contains only two items—understaffed centers and cramped office space—this imbalance may be a key source of stress for you and your colleagues.

Balancing Work and Personal Life

Live a balanced life-

Learn some and think some and draw and paint some

And sing and dance and play and work every day some.

—Robert Fulghum

Most people work for two reasons: to support themselves and their families, and to contribute something of value to the world. Do you ever feel like earning your paycheck doesn't leave you enough time and energy to spend with your family or in your own personal endeavors?

Your days at work are long and filled with demands, and yet it may be difficult to justify going home at a reasonable hour when there is still important work left to be done. Perhaps you were at a meeting the night before, so you could even leave early, but you tend to "just keep going." This type of behavior isn't good for you, for your personal or family life, or even for your organization.

Keeping your life in balance is difficult, especially if you have a strong work ethic, but you'll benefit from your efforts to achieve a healthy balance. A satisfying personal life can help you keep the frustrations at work in perspective and give you the energy to meet another challenging day. Likewise, having a fulfilling job can help you cope with the normal frustrations of family life. The skills you develop at work can help you at home, and the empathy and insight you develop as a member of your own family can help you be more effective in your job. If you don't care for yourself, you have less to give on the job. Being an active part of your family and community makes you a better leader.

Here are some things you can think about and do to balance work and family life:

- Take a personal inventory of what is working well in your work and family/personal life right now; count your "blessings" and your strengths.
- Note the things that you wish you could change.
- Ask others to share home chores or outside commitments (call a family meeting to discuss dividing up routine household tasks).
- Don't blame yourself for every personal difficulty. Your "real life" problems are ones that many families face.
- If the workload is just too great, consider communicating your challenges to your supervisor, board, and elected officials; join with others to work collectively toward solutions. For example, explore the possibility of increasing staffing for your program or department.

Bara Litman, Program Manager of the Massachusetts Institute of Technology Work-Life Center, suggests some mini-strategies for creating a better internal balance:[29]

- *Breathing and Focus*: Three times a day, take three breaths following these steps:
- Breathe in (count "1, 2, 3, 4").
- Hold (for a count of "1").
- Breathe out (count from 1 to 8, slowly and steadily, with pursed lips, as if blowing through a straw).
- Hold (for a count of "1"). Repeat two more times.
- Check your pulse to see if the breathing has reduced your heart rate. Deep breathing can slow down the flight or fight response.
- *Three Good Things*: Each day, write down three good things that happened to you or went well that day. Reflect on why they went well. Writing these things down every day helps to train your mind to remember the positive things when you're focused on the negative. It also helps you to appreciate the small things that contribute to well-being along with the big things.
- *Ask for Help*: At home or work, it's okay to ask for help. Delegating teaches others important skills and builds confidence. Relinquishing some control may be difficult at first; however, asking for help can reduce stress and provide you with quality time for other things.
- *Say No*: We can't say yes to everything. If it's something you really don't need or want to do, respectfully say no.

- Maintain personal balance, even when others around you are unbalanced.
- Count to 24. Waiting 24 hours before reacting gives you time to reflect and gain perspective.
- Don't make assumptions.
- Who is the cheerleader at home or in your personal life?
- Take a break.
- Have a ritual for leaving work *at* work.
- Don't sweat the small stuff.
- Decrease your whining, increase your gratitude.
- "Remember that you become what you practice the most."[30]

Creating your own stress reduction and wellness program

Forward thinking employers realize that employees perform best when both their personal and their professional lives are going well. Find out if your organization or health insurance plan offers health and wellness programs; if neither does, find ways to create your own.

Stress is a response that varies with each person and circumstance. The effects of chronic stress have been proven to be uniformly detrimental to long-term health and well-being. There are two types of stress: positive and negative. You might experience positive stress when you become a new parent or send your first child off to college. You're likely to experience negative stress when you're faced with sudden illness or the prospect of layoffs or funding cuts.

The following analogy may help you distinguish between positive and negative stress:

> As a potter presses clay on a spinning wheel, a shape begins to emerge. The rotation of the pottery wheel and the gentle, yet firm hands of the potter work together to mold a mass of clay into a beautiful form. If the potter exerts too much pressure the clay will break or tear. If the potter exerts too little pressure, the clay will not transform into a piece of pottery. After the potter is done making the pot, the clay must "rest" before being fired. Like clay pots or vases, we can become our best when we experience enough stress, but not too much. We also need time to rest, especially before and after times of "fire" in our lives.

Following are some elements of a balanced personal stress reduction and wellness program.

Daily mindfulness practice

Refer to earlier sections of this chapter to help you design and implement a daily mindfulness practice that's comfortable and manageable for you.

Exercise you enjoy enough to actually do

Exercise not only keeps you fit (and better able to handle stress); it also reduces the effects of stress and enhances brain health. Here are three approaches you could take to exercise:

1. *The easy-going approach*: Build some moderate, fun exercise into your life several times a week. Take the stairs instead of the elevator. On a nice day, walk to a park and eat your lunch. In the evening, before going to bed, try a warm shower and ten minutes of easy stretching. Sign up for a beginning yoga or dance class.

2. *The take-it-seriously approach*: Consult your doctor first, then jump headlong into a serious exercise program that burns calories, tightens up your muscles, and increases your cardiovascular strength. Set

challenging but reachable goals. Join a fitness center, engage a trainer, or sign up for a class that meets often and spurs you on.

3. *The wait-and-see approach*: Read a magazine or watch a TV program about exercise. Listen to your doctor tell you that you should lose some weight. Think about exercising but be too busy with work demands or family commitments that you avoid doing it. Then have a sudden, serious health problem, become highly motivated, and proceed to steps 1 and 2 above.

People who routinely practice a regime of exercise, strength training, and/or meditation to help mitigate stress often describe a feeling of inner elation or euphoria during and right after doing so. This state of deep, unconscious awareness and presence in the moment occurs when the body produces its own natural painkillers, called endorphins, which block pain and produce a feeling of wellness.

Eat healthy foods that you actually enjoy

Some foods reduce stress, while other foods exacerbate it. Whole grains, fruits, and vegetables help you maintain balanced energy and feel good. High-fat, fried foods, soda, and sweets can make you gain weight, feel jittery, and contribute to heart disease and diabetes. Skipping meals or consuming too much caffeine (coffee, chocolate, tea, colas) can increase your stress level. High-carbohydrate foods such as white bread, pasta, cookies, and other sweets are sometimes called "comfort foods." They may make you feel good momentarily because they rapidly increase your blood sugar; but they actually make you feel tired soon after your blood sugar level drops. Eating quickly at your desk can add to your stress, and eating while driving can be dangerous to yourself and others.

Try an experiment for a week: Write down everything you eat and drink and how you feel each day. Once you see what you usually eat and how it affects you, then you can decide whether you want to make some changes. If you do try some new ways of eating, notice how you feel after eating each new food.

If it's not realistic to give up soda or comfort foods "cold turkey," you can become more aware of how they create or reduce stress in your life. Notice what you choose to eat at the office or during conferences. Try choosing a piece of fruit instead of a pastry at the next meeting you attend. Plan to gradually limit caffeine intake. Every way you choose to be kind to your body reduces stress and enhances your overall health and well-being.

Friends and family

One of the best ways to handle work is to get away from it. Honor your feelings when you feel "stressed out." Step out of your leadership role and take a break. "Check in" with your partner, child, or a friend. Family members and friends can become so accustomed to your "not right now, maybe later" commitment to work that they stop asking for your time and attention. Then, when you come up for a "breather" and want to spend some time with loved ones, they've usually already filled their time with other commitments.

Family members and good friends are often the unsung heroes behind successful leaders. The unrelenting pace of a leader's work may leave little time to nurture relationships. Ask yourself: "How much has work drawn me away from my family and friends recently?" Consider scheduling one evening each week just for time with family or friends. Caring for friends and loved ones who take care of you is not about what you can provide with your paycheck; it's about giving them the most precious gift—your time, attention, and love.

Harmful habits and addictions

Many people seek to numb the pain and distress in their lives by using or abusing drugs or alcohol, smoking cigarettes, gambling, eating, or shopping compulsively. Sometimes it's very hard to recognize when you have crossed the line from user to abuser, especially if a harmful habit has numbed or distorted your perceptions. If you use alcohol or go shopping for things you don't need whenever you feel discouraged, then you might not be facing whatever it is that's making you feel so sad, frustrated, or hopeless. Feeling your emotions is essential to living life fully. If you're angry, it's healthier to express your anger—respectfully and safely—than to ignore it.

If you're hiding your habits or addictions from others, or if people who love you have asked you to get help, pay attention and listen! If you have the courage to face a harmful habit or addiction and work through the recovery process, you'll be far more effective in your work and be able to live a healthier, happier life.

Counseling

There are times when it's helpful to have a skillful "outsider" with whom to talk to about life's inevitable problems and challenges. Going for professional counseling can sometimes be hard to do, especially if you feel you should "have it all together." Keep in mind that most people, including counselors themselves, can benefit from seeing a counselor at certain times in their lives. Doing so is a sign of strength and wisdom to recognize that you need help.

When you call a counseling service, you might be told there's a waiting list; go ahead and reserve a spot if you're comfortable waiting for an appointment. You can request to be seen immediately, however, if you're feeling very anxious or distressed. All reputable counseling services are able to find a counselor to see you right away should the need arise.

Your employer may offer an Employee Assistance Program (EAP) as a benefit. An EAP usually works with a local counseling service to provide short-term professional counseling at little or no cost. This service is strictly confidential. Your employer will not be notified as to why you've come for counseling. If your employer has an EAP, your family members can probably use it as well.

Your employer, the EAP program, or another community group may also offer free or inexpensive support groups for people with common, challenging life circumstances, such as providing care for elderly parents, coping with loss and grief, or parenting a troubled teenager. Participating in such a group can provide great support, as you get to know people with similar concerns and are able to share your struggles, and come up with creative and practical solutions.

---

[22] Daniel J. Siegal, *Mind: A Journey to the Heart of Being Human*. (New York: W. W. Norton, 2016).

[23] Ellen Langer, *Mindfulness* (Read, MA: Perseus, 1989); Ellen Langer, *The Power of Mindful Learning* (Reading, MA: Perseus, 1997).

[24] Janice Marturano, *Finding the Space to Lead: A Practical Guide to Mindful Leadership* (London: Bloomsbury, 2014).

[25] William Duggan, *Strategic Intuition: The Creative Spark in Human Achievement* (New York: Columbia Business School, 2013); William Duggan, *Creative Strategy: A Guide for Innovation* (New York: Columbia Business School, 2014).

[26] Marturano, *Finding the Space to Lead*, 29.

[27] Salli Rasberry and Padi Selwyn, *Living Your Life Out Loud: How to Unlock Your Creativity and Unleash Your Joy* (New York: Pocket Books, 1981).

[28] The Family Circles Assessment is adapted from the Cornell Empowerment Group's Social Ecological Model, the Social World model developed by Moncrieff Cochran, and Urie Bronfenbrenner's Ecological model.

[29] Adapted from Bara Litman, "Rebalancing Work & Life: Be the Model" (Webinar: Military Families Learning Network, 2018).

[30] Richard Carlson, *Don't Sweat the Small Stuff* (New York: Hachette, 1997), 171-72.

Chapter 3—Additional Resources

Books

Campbell, T. Colin, and Thomas M. Campbell. *The China Study: Startling Implications for Diet, Weight Loss and Long-term health*. Dallas: BenBella, 2006.

Carlson, Richard. *Don't Sweat the Small Stuff … and It's All Small Stuff: Simple Ways to keep the Little Things from Taking Over Your Life*. New York: Hachette, 1997.

Goleman, Daniel. *Focus: The Hidden Driver of Excellence*, New York: Harper, 2012.

Kabat-Zinn, Jon. *Full Catastrophe Living: Using the Wisdom of Your Body and Mind to Face Stress, Pain, and Illness*. New York: Delta, 1990.

Kabat-Zin, Jon. *The Healing Power of Mindfulness: A New Way of Being*. New York: Hatchette, 2018.

Kabat-Zinn, Jon. *Mindfulness for All: The Wisdom to Transform the World*. London: Piatkus, 2019.

Kabat-Zinn, M., and Jon Kabat-Zinn. *Everyday Blessings: The Inner Work of Mindful Parenting*. New York: Hyperion, 1997.

Langer, E. *Mindfulness*. Reading, MA: Perseus, 1989.

Langer, E. *The Power of Mindful Learning*. Reading, MA: Perseus, 1997.

Lipman-Blumen, J. *The Connective Edge: Leading in an Interdependent World*. San Francisco: Jossey-Bass, 1996.

Marturano, Janice. *Finding the Space to Lead: A Practical Guide to Mindful Leadership*. New York: Bloomsbury, 2014.

Muth, Jon J. *Zen Shorts*. New York: Scholastic, 2005.

Rasberry, S., and P. Selwyn. *Living Your Life Out Loud: How to Unlock Your Creativity and Unleash your Joy*. New York: Pocket Books, 1981.

Rechtschaffen, S. *Time Shifting: Creating More Time for Your Life*. New York: Doubleday, 1997.

Santorelli, S. *Heal Thyself: Lessons on Mindfulness in Medicine*. New York: Bell Tower, 1999.

Siegal, Daniel J. *Mind: A Journey to the Heart of Being Human*. New York: W. W. Norton, 2016.

Williams, Mark, John Teasdale, Zindel V. Segal, and Jon Kabat-Zinn. *The Mindful Way Through Depression: Freeing Yourself from Chronic Unhappiness*. New York: Guildford, 2007.

Articles

Killingsworth, Matt. "Does Mind Wandering Make you Unhappy?" *Greater Good Magazine* (online, July 16, 2013). https://greatergood.berkeley.edu/article/item/does_mind_wandering_make_you_unhappy.

Diener, Ed, and Martin E. P. Seligman. "Very Happy People." *Psychological Science* 13, no. 1 (2002). https://doi.org/10.1111%2F1467-9280.00415.

Recordings and websites

Santorelli, Saki. "The Healing Practice of Mindfulness with Saki Santorelli." Berlin: Better Listen!, 2014.

Frantic World. "Mindfulness: Finding Peace in a Frantic World—Free Meditations from Mindfulness." http://franticworld.com/free-meditations-from-mindfulness.

UCLA Mindfulness Awareness Research Center. Podcasts. http://www.mindful.org/.

Psychology Today. "Mindfulness." https://www.psychologytoday.com/us/basics/mindfulness.

UMass Center for Mindfulness. http://www.umassmed.edu/cfm/.

Ideas for Independent Learning Projects

Following are suggestions for independent learning projects to help you reflect on the supervisory and personal leadership theories and strategies for self-empowerment presented in this chapter. *We encourage you to develop your own independent learning project that's relevant to your workplace, or make modifications to the ones listed below, to create a meaningful and manageable plan.*

- Write a reflection on your vision as a supervisor or leader; include thoughts on the adapted FDC Core Principles for leaders and supervisors, and the supervision and leadership theories that align with family development. Discuss why you entered your field of work, how and why you decided to become a supervisor or leader, and what people, events, or circumstances have shaped your leadership approach. Describe what you need to do to move your vision to the next step and how you plan to implement it.

- Focus one workday's routine to include the theme of mindfulness. Develop a plan that includes your own version of incorporating mindfulness into the workday. At home that night, try out one or more of the techniques for mindful breathing, walking, listening, or stretching. Prepare a plan for observing your workplace and natural environment, and interacting in mindful ways with co-workers, families, and colleagues for a day. Write a reflection about what you did, how it felt, and how others responded when you carried out your plan.

- If your agency doesn't have a code of ethics, use the FDC Code as a springboard to help your agency develop one. Coordinate the steps in a plan for leaders and staff members to review the FDC Code, meet to discuss their ideas, and prepare a draft code of ethics customized for your agency. Write a reflection on this process and how you feel leadership and self-empowerment contribute to creating and sustaining an ethical workplace.

- Facilitate the adaptation of the Family Circles Assessment as a reflective activity at an upcoming staff meeting. Draw the circles on a large piece of paper, and adapt the categories to reflect elements in the "family circle" of your organization. Spend a few minutes after the assessment is complete to elicit feedback on the strengths and stressors of your workplace. Listen for ways that you, as a leader, can help balance supports or reduce stressors. Write a reflection on how the activity went and what you learned from staff, and describe what you'll do as a leader to promote empowerment in your organization.

- Develop a personal stress reduction and wellness plan using some of the ideas and strategies from this chapter. Use the plan over the next 30 days. Include a variety of self-empowerment strategies, and keep track of your progress. After 30 days, write a reflection on how it went, what worked, what didn't work, and what you plan to do as a result of this exercise.

Chapter 4
Supervising with Skill and Heart

Learning objectives

- Use "peripheral vision" to see the strengths in staff members to better establish and build mutually respectful relationships.

- Expand your vision to see the "bigger picture" in goal setting and strategic planning.

- Determine how much personal information to share with staff members.

- Understand how to support staff during major organizational transitions.

- Increase awareness of and help staff manage workplace stress and job "burnout."

- Seek support in helping staff cope with traumatic events.

- Practice conflict resolution skills using the principles and practices of family development.

- Understand the dynamics of group development in the workplace.

- Use creative discussion techniques in staff meetings and with other groups.

Staying focused on the "vision" of supervision

Supervising with "skill and heart" means adopting a balanced and comprehensive approach to handling both the routine and the challenging aspects of supervision. As a leader, you know that supervising others is an extremely important part of your job. Through observation, communication, facilitation, and at times, conflict resolution, you strive to balance the needs and abilities of your staff members with the demands of meeting agency goals.

Supervising with a balance of skill and heart is an art and a science. The "science" of supervision is to break down complex projects into manageable tasks by delegating responsibilities and providing the tools to get the job done. The "art" of supervision is to create new possibilities and innovative solutions to problems by sharing and combining resources. This chapter offers practical techniques and strategies to help you become a more effective supervisor.

In *Empowerment Skills for Family Workers*, participants learn the concept of developing "bifocal vision": the ability to see at two levels at the same time. Through bifocal vision, a worker can see the reality of a family's current situation, and at the same time see their natural strengths and resources.

Just as it's important for workers to develop bifocal vision in helping families, it's equally important for supervisors to develop this ability in working with staff members. For example, you may supervise an individual who you consider to be stubborn and opinionated, but you may also be able to see how their strong work ethic contributes to your agency's effectiveness.

It's a challenge to balance the reality of a staff member's attitudes, work habits, and relationships with others, with the desire to help that individual and all other staff members recognize and build on their individual and collective strengths. Many people are so accustomed to seeing their deficits that they may not believe you when you reflect a strength back to them. Your *own* commitment to the belief that all workers have strengths is your most powerful tool in building mutually respectful relationships with those you supervise.

Another way to identify strengths in your staff members is to use "peripheral vision": the ability to observe and find strengths, similarities, and common ground with those you supervise. For example, try taking a walk through your agency office space as if you were a visitor. Observe individual workspaces and take note of the photographs, posters, and other personal items you see. These are clues to guide you in finding common ground with those you supervise. These "artifacts" can tell you a great deal about how your staff members feel about their work and their lives.

On the next page is a sketch of a typical worker's desk at a family support agency. Look over the drawing using your peripheral vision. Generate a mental list of what you think this worker values, and then identify areas of common ground that might help you develop a more effective working relationship with this individual.

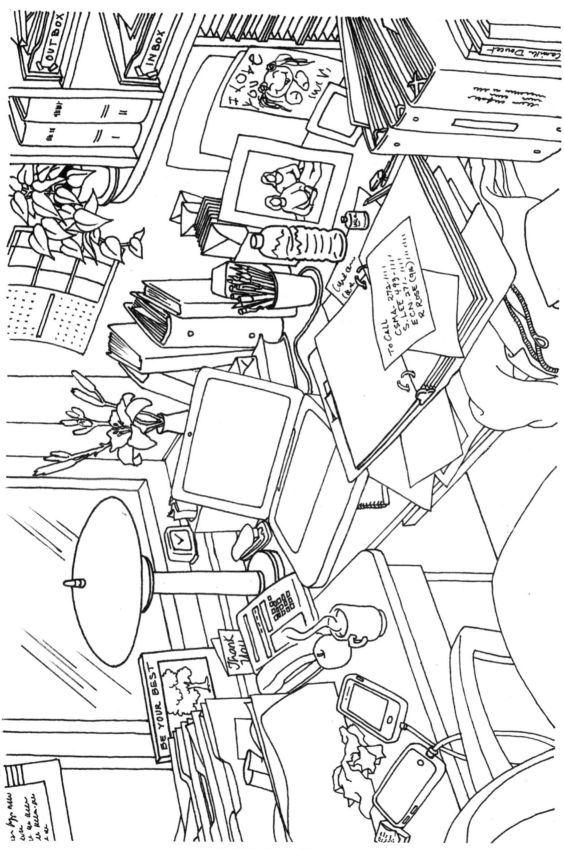

© 2019 Claire Forest

A third type of vision is "tunnel" vision: the inability to see the peripheral or broader perspective. You may be using tunnel vision if you allow unimportant details or events to consume excessive amounts of your energy. For example, if one of your staff members tells you at the last minute that they can't attend a scheduled meeting because of a family emergency, your tunnel vision may cause you to respond with anger rather than empathy. A broader perspective could help you realize that family workers frequently have to juggle conflicting demands between home and work. As a supervisor, you need to support your staff members and help them plan and achieve goals, just as you do with your agency's families.

Leaders with tunnel vision are often too focused on fitting one piece into the organizational puzzle. Here are two steps you can take to avoid tunnel vision:

1. At the end of each month, reflect on the important projects or programs, and ask yourself: How effectively did I spend my time in addressing long-term goals and priorities?

2. Listen thoughtfully to suggestions, and incorporate recommendations that you believe will improve the final product of your work. You'll benefit from the insights you gain through a broader, collaborative perspective.

Another approach to supervision that can help you avoid "tunnel" vision and at the same time develop your critical thinking skills is called "reflecting-in-action."[31] This is the habit of reflecting *during* an interaction or situation to understand how your beliefs or values are affecting a goal. There are times when you need to step back from your work to look at things from a "bird's-eye" view. From that vantage point, you can begin to see the interconnectedness and interdependency among services, programs, and systems.

Developing mutually respectful relationships

In previous chapters, you learned that the family development model is practiced and based on the principle that healthy self-reliance and empowerment develops when people identify, choose, and set their own goals. Using the family development model, supervisors can develop relationships with workers that provide guidance and direction, while still supporting a worker's need for healthy self-reliance in setting their own personal and professional goals.

In Chapter 2, you learned about the value of role models in life and work. Along with acting as a role model to those you supervise, you may also wish to consider being a mentor. A mentor is a person with trustworthy knowledge and experience, or specialized training, who encourages the development of a less experienced person entering a trade or profession. In today's vernacular, the term "mentor" is more often used to describe a person's genuine interest in and concern for the well-being of someone else. The role of a mentor, according to Laurent Daloz, author of the book *Mentor: Guiding the Journey of Adult Learners*,[32] is to foster the development of the *whole* person through a relationship process. Mentors can be of any gender, race, spirituality, age, socio-economic status, or culture. Supervisors, teachers, coaches, spiritual leaders, colleagues, and even parents can serve as mentors.

You may want to develop relationships with workers in mentor-like ways that promote and encourage their personal and career development. But perhaps you are concerned that your interest might be misconstrued or manipulated if you inquire too much or too curiously about their life outside of work. You may be uncomfortable asking about a worker's future goals and dreams if you're not willing to share similar information with them. Moreover, if you know a lot about a worker's personal difficulties and those problems begin to affect their work performance, you may feel guilty when you need to impose more stringent professional boundaries in the relationship.

How much of your own personal life should you share with your staff members? Some staff may share a lot of personal information with you. They may think the relationship is one-sided unless you share personal information as well. Here are some guidelines to help you answer this question:

- Be genuine.

- Offer empathy and share your own personal experiences to build rapport. For example, if a staff member is struggling to help their aging mother decide whether to return home after a serious fall, you could say, "That must be a really difficult decision for you and your mother. I can really relate to your dilemma because my mother had a serious operation last year. Tell me more about your mother's situation."

- Don't rely on your co-workers or staff to help you solve your problems. Set up a good support system for yourself so you don't become dependent on those you work with. When you gain insight into your own life through your work relationship (as you certainly will), or when co-workers take on some of your work in an emergency, do thank them for the ways in which they helped you.

- Be prepared for anything you share to be discussed (and possibly distorted) by others. For example, if you tell a co-worker the details of your personal struggles with your teenager, you need to accept that this information may not be held in confidence.

- Share enough personal information for co-workers to see that you're "real," but not so much that you become dependent on their discretion to keep important confidences.

If those you supervise are FDC-credentialed, they should have a strong foundation in communicating effectively, and in the principles of developing mutually respectful relationships. When both leaders and staff participate in empowerment-based training such as FDC, and learn to communicate more skillfully through listening well, paraphrasing, feedback, and "I" messages, the entire organization experiences positive outcomes.

Guidelines for strengths-based assessment with workers

From the time social service programs were introduced at the turn of the last century, the traditional method of measuring the success of a program or agency was to compile information about the number of services provided. For some time now, there has been a shift to assess the benefits of programs using a goals-based or "outcomes-measurement" approach.

Models of outcomes-measurement assessment, such as the United Way's Strengthening Families' Logic Model,[33] are currently used by many organizations. In the past, the goal of traditional evaluation methods was to provide grand-scale "totals" in annual reports showing an increasingly higher (or lower) number of services provided, according to overall program goals. The goal of today's outcomes-measurement assessment is to project outcomes of services and goals, and to measure and report progress on an incremental or periodic basis. In addition, these incremental reports include information regarding program strengths in overcoming unforeseen obstacles and anecdotes about families' efforts and successes.

Outcomes-measurement assessment has been a positive innovation for most family support organizations because it has helped funders and agencies work more collaboratively in understanding the resources and processes needed for family development. However, outcomes-measurement assessment is inadequate as a sole method of evaluation for assessment *within* the organization, for these reasons:

- Assessing the outcomes of a worker's or team's efforts by projecting the numbers of families served does not give a true indication of family's success or satisfaction with services.

- There's no way to show how workers or teams have overcome obstacles to achieve outcomes and unanticipated goals.

- The predetermined and linear process of this assessment doesn't readily allow for a "loop of learning" through feedback and reflection by workers, the team, and supervisors.

How can you assess the efforts and competencies of workers and teams in ways that recognize individual differences, and yet apply consistent standards? You can use *strengths-based* assessment to help you focus on the strengths of workers (and teams) in measuring program and agency outcomes. If you're required to use standardized assessment forms, such as an annual performance review, you could also use the following guidelines to collect information that reflects a strengths-based approach. If your agency develops its own program assessment and performance review tools, you can use these guidelines to revise the forms to gather strengths-based information.

Here are our recommendations for using strengths-based assessment with workers:

1. Collect the information you need to assess a worker's or team's efforts and outcomes through a variety of sources (i.e., visit a worker/team in their natural work setting, attend a meeting, and if possible, periodically arrange to observe a worker interacting with a family or work group). Include a self-assessment as part of the process.

2. Help the worker/team identify a major goal, along with steps that both of you will take to achieve that goal. This allows you to collect information about strengths and resources as you observe them negotiate obstacles and complete steps toward a goal.

3. Assess the worker's/team's performance according to criteria that you've developed together and know in advance.

4. Approach performance review of staff/team members with a strengths-based point of view, recognizing each person's natural strengths and resources, seeing difficulties as opportunities to learn, and helping them develop skills and apply them to current and future practice.

5. When areas of improvement are indicated, ask what you can do to help support the worker/team in their efforts.

Supporting staff through transitions such as reductions, cutbacks and reorganization

All organizations experience change over time, and the ebb and flow of staffing, funding, or restructuring can affect staff morale. Widespread or dramatic organizational changes such as layoffs and job cuts can profoundly affect the emotional resources of an agency. Restructuring divisions or departments, even if change is announced and phased in over time, can be unsettling and disorienting for many staff members. You can build in ways to support your staff during these times of change by understanding the complex ways that individuals respond to loss.

Most everyone experiences "minor" daily losses, such as having to leave a child at daycare or cancelling lunch with a good friend. However, coping with a major loss such as losing a job, a child leaving home, or the death of a loved one requires a process of transition. Even merely moving to a new office within the same building can create a sense of loss.

When people face life's deepest losses and disappointments, they go through a period of grief and mourning that's complex and highly individual. The adjustment to major life-altering loss is generally a process of stages. While theories explaining the grief and mourning process vary, most identify the following stages:

- A period of denial and disbelief, including physical symptoms that personalize the loss
- Expressions of sadness, guilt, relief, despair, hopelessness, anger, and finally acceptance
- Attempts to memorialize the loss while beginning to reach out to others and establish new relationships
- Lifelong adjustment with cycles of grief if new losses reawaken areas of grieving that are incomplete

The following model illustrates the typical grief process:

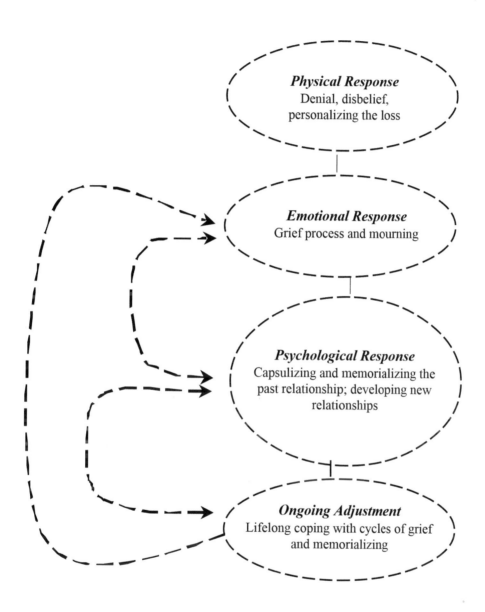

Grief is a normal, natural response to loss; however, there are sometimes situations that can interfere with a person's ability to express the normal responses to personal loss. *Disenfranchised grief* is a term coined by gerontologist and minister Kenneth Doka describing the experience of personal loss that, for whatever reason, can't be publicly acknowledged, mourned, and supported.[34]

The following types of organizational changes are examples of situations in which individuals may experience disenfranchised grief:

- Terminations, lay-offs, or "incentive" early retirements that eliminate working relationships
- Reorganization that changes well-established relationships with supervisors

- Promotions that change a worker's role from peer to supervisor of former co-workers
- High-staff-turnover situations that require remaining workers to constantly adjust to loss and change
- Relocations or transfers that disrupt workers or make it difficult for them to maintain close relationships with former colleagues
- Unexpected building closure or demolition due to natural disasters
- Widespread tragedy or trauma that undermines a worker's sense of normalcy

When layoffs or cutbacks occur, those workers not affected may feel guilty for having been "spared." When agencies restructure through reorganization and redirect well-established groups and lines of authority, workers may lose their sense of identity and belonging. The patience and responsiveness of supervisors during this type of change can be tremendously important to workers adjusting to loss. Staff members may feel that if they openly discuss or ask questions about the transition/loss, then they'll be labeled as "whiners" or "troublemakers." To keep the agency moving forward, leaders may want to downplay the event publicly to avoid further explanation and embarrassment. At these times, decisions about what information to share and what staff can expect in the future can be very sensitive.

If you're a supervisor or leader who's already experienced supporting staff through a major loss at your organization, you have insight that can help in this area. For others, we offer these suggestions:

- Be aware of and responsive to the grief process that workers and teams experience as a result of a major transition or loss.
- Help staff express their feelings about the impact of the loss on them and the organization, and provide practical assistance to make the transition smoother.
- Offer hope and encouragement wherever you can to help staff members regain a sense of stability.
- Expect disruption and confusion in worker and team performance immediately before and after a major transition.

As important as it is to be sensitive to staff members during these difficult times, you may also be personally involved and deeply affected through this process. You may have advance information on a major change and have to tell very competent and caring staff members that their jobs have been cut. If you're on the front line of an organization during a major transition, staff members may project their anger about the situation onto you. You may feel disenfranchised in your own grief about the changes happening in your organization. Refer to Chapter 3: Leadership and Self-Empowerment to review ways to help yourself reclaim strategies to support yourself during stressful times.

Helping staff manage workplace stress

The chronic effects of even moderate workplace stress can deplete the vital physical and emotional reserves of staff members. Family-serving organizations exist to provide services and support in response to society's most disturbing problems: homelessness, malnutrition, communicable disease, domestic violence, neglect and abuse of children and adults, alcohol and substance abuse, and mental illness. Front-line workers who visit families in their homes may observe unsafe and unhealthy conditions, even violence and abuse. Even workers who feel they've become desensitized to the heartbreaking plight of some families can be shocked when one of their families experiences a catastrophe.

Workers with less experience, or who have several families in crisis at the same time, can become overwhelmed. The experience of observing or witnessing the pain, suffering and trauma of others is termed vicarious trauma.[35] Family workers who are habitually exposed to the chronic hardships of families can begin to feel powerless and traumatized, especially when a shocking tragedy occurs.

As a supervisor, you can help your staff members manage the effects of vicarious trauma with a technique called *reframing*, which is a way to help a person revise a negative or self-defeating opinion or feeling. Try this:

1. Place the tips of your index fingers and thumbs together in front of your eyes to create a "frame."

2. Narrow the focus of your vision to look through your frame and focus on an object. The frame you've created accentuates that object and allows you to focus on its characteristics (its assets and flaws) in greater detail.

3. Once you take your fingers down, the object becomes a part of the larger picture again.

The flaws you observed under close scrutiny may not have the same impact when you view the object within a larger setting. Reframing can help you to redirect your focus from negative to positive aspects and view one situation or event in perspective, so that you see it as part of a larger picture.

In the book, *Counseling Adults in Transition: Linking Practice with Theory*,[36] Schlossber, Water, and Goodman describe three types of situations in which reframing is helpful. They describe when someone:

- Overgeneralizes what they know from one situation to their view of other, or all, situations
- Changes their thoughts or feelings about a situation to justify a negative outcome
- Selectively omits information that would ameliorate—or introduce a positive element into—a negative experience

Here are examples of each type of situation where reframing can be used in response:

Overgeneralizing from one situation

Statement: "That agency isn't helpful. The last time I called there, the worker didn't help me."

Reframing response: "Maybe the worker was having a bad day. I know the agency has been around for a long time and I've heard they have a good reputation in the community."

Justifying a negative event

Statement: "He must have been driving too fast or else he wouldn't have had an accident."

Reframing response: "It's fortunate that he was wearing his seat belt and didn't get seriously injured."

Leaving out positive aspects

Statement: "The agency didn't give us the raise we were promised."

Reframing response: "However, I heard the agency is still going to contribute to our 401K accounts and that raises will be considered again in six months."

By using the technique of reframing, you can help staff manage the effects of stress and vicarious trauma by helping them recognize that negative situations or events can reveal underlying strengths, and offering hope that the efforts they make today will be appreciated and produce positive change in the future.

Reframing is a useful technique for supporting everyone in your organization by reducing anxiety and modeling empathy. Here's an acronym to help you remember and share the reframing approach:

REFRAMING

ENCOURAGES

FOCUS,

REDUCES

ANXIETY,

MODELS

EMPATHY

Recognizing symptoms of job "burnout"

Many human service professionals have an intellectual understanding that they don't need to "fix" others' problems, but in their hearts they still want to. Some relationships thrive with just a minimum of support during rough times; others require more "hands on" guidance and direction. It's important that you balance your desire to help a staff member develop self-reliance with your inclination to provide daily oversight and guidance. If a supervisor offers too much help, a worker can feel disempowered and, over time, resentful. If a supervisor offers too little help, a worker can feel overwhelmed and unable to function.

A recent Gallup poll of nearly 7,500 full-time employees found that 23% reported feeling "burned out" at work very often or always. An additional 44% reported feeling burned out sometimes. Two thirds of the full-time workers in this study experienced some level of "burnout,"[37] a term first coined in the 1970s by American psychologist Herbert Freudenberger in referring to the stress and exhaustion felt by those in helping professions like doctors and nurses that make it tough for them to cope. While job burnout is certainly prevalent in the helping professions, it can occur in any employment situation.

In the Gallup study, primary reasons given by workers experiencing high levels of stress contributing to job burnout were unfair treatment at work, unmanageable workloads, lack of support from managers and the added stress of having to respond to emails and texts during off hours. The American Institute of Stress also cites a survey indicating main sources of stress for workers[38]:

- Juggling work and personal lives: 20%
- Lack of job security: 6%
- People issues: 28%
- Workload: 46%

There's a real cost to job burnout in the workplace. It contributes to high levels of absenteeism and turnover. The *Harvard Business Review* reported that job burnout also accounts for an estimated $125 to $190 billion in health care spending. Chronic stress can be a contributing factor for coronary heart disease, gastrointestinal issues, high cholesterol, and even type 2 diabetes, in addition to the emotional toll it often takes.

Job burnout is a harsh reality today. While there is stress in every job, the cumulative effect on every woman, man, and child in this country can be alarming. Burnout is a condition that, over time, results in people becoming so stressed, dissatisfied, pessimistic, and fatigued that their abilities to perform their routine work duties become hindered or impaired. It's important to realize that everyone is susceptible to job burnout—including you—but there are often warning signs to look for.

Low energy and feelings of extreme tiredness are often experienced in the early stages of burnout. In the later stages, just *thinking* about work may be stressful; reluctance to go to work may result in frequent absenteeism.

As time goes on, another symptom of burnout is increased cynicism and decreased empathy.[39] A loss of enjoyment in one's work and feelings of pessimism can result in detachment from program participants. This feeling of detachment can in turn lead to withdrawal from activities previously enjoyed outside of work.

In the later stages of burnout, workers may feel unable to do their job effectively. These feelings of apathy can result in lack of effort, ultimately impacting their job performance.

Here are ways to determine if you or a staff member is at more than average risk for job burnout:

- Ongoing, excessive workloads (having too much to do in too little time, or consistently being required to perform at peak capacity without adjustments being made in other duties)
- Life-altering stresses in non-work areas that consume time and emotional energy
- Working an excessive number of hours each week
- Work duties that significantly underutilize a person's skills and abilities
- Sedentary jobs or jobs that require more physical strength than a person can manage on a daily basis
- Jobs with unclear expectations and unpredictable measures of accountability for results
- Working in a physically or emotionally stressful workplace without having power to change the environment

You can help staff members and colleagues who you feel are at risk for job burnout in practical and supportive ways:

- When hiring new staff or assigning responsibilities, consider the skill set and job fit for the employee. Getting to know the strengths of each staff member allows you to better assign tasks and set goals that are manageable and achievable.
- Consult with staff in identifying areas and topics where staff could benefit from additional training and support. Self-assessment is essential to growth, and the acquisition of knowledge and new skills.
- Foster strong partnerships and positive relationships in the workplace. Having co-workers you can rely on and being a reliable partner builds in return a cohesive team and strong support network.
- Give staff opportunities to grow and be successful. Jobs that underutilize skills or become too routine or repetitive can lead to a lack of interest or apathy.
- Communicate. Effective managers are open to discussing a worker's situation, supporting them through difficult times, and working collaboratively to address the stressors that may be causing burnout.

The process outlined in the next section can be helpful in knowing when staff members need additional support and in creating a manageable workload to prevent burnout.

Seven Steps of Family Development adapted for a supervisor-worker relationship

The following seven steps of family development can be a useful guide, even though you may not use all of them, or even in this exact order. Once you've taken the initial step of supporting a worker, you do need to follow up with an approach that balances responsibility and autonomy.

1. A supervisor develops a partnership with a worker.
2. A supervisor helps the worker assess their needs and strengths. This is an ongoing process.

3. A supervisor and worker set goals together and collaboratively identify ideas for achieving them.

4. A supervisor helps a worker make a plan to achieve the goals with some of the tasks being the responsibility of the worker and some the responsibility of the supervisor.

5. The supervisor and worker learn and practice skills needed to be inter-reliant. This is an ongoing process.

6. The supervisor and worker collaborate using services as stepping stones to help reach goals.

7. A healthy balance between the supervisor's and worker's sense of responsibility is restored. The organization is strengthened through the process and the supervisor and worker are better able to handle future challenges.

Responsibility and autonomy are the building blocks of your partnership with workers. For workers to trust that their efforts can produce worthwhile results, they need personal skills and abilities, good training and clear expectations. You can help your staff members successfully balance responsibility and accountability through appropriate follow-up. You need to provide complete information about assignments, expectations, and deadlines. *You can achieve this balance best when you set goals and work collaboratively.*

Handling trauma in the workplace

Some professions, such as law enforcement, abuse and crisis intervention, emergency medicine, and the military expose workers to elements of the darkest side of humanity every day. People who work in these occupations must be trained to protect themselves, and to seek professional help with the inevitable stress of such dangerous work. There are times when a personal tragedy can debilitate an individual's emotional capacity to handle routine stress. There are also times when a calamity of such intensity and magnitude occurs that its effect can traumatize workers, teams, an entire agency—or even an entire community.

In recent years, it seems that hardly a week or month goes by without reports of mass shootings, terrorist attacks, or other gun violence. It can feel as though these attacks could happen anywhere and at any time, resulting in uncertainty and fear. Climate change has also contributed to extreme weather events such as hurricanes, floods, and wildfires, any of which can leave devastation in their wake.

The following are situations in which the risk of traumatic stress is highest:

- Personal and family catastrophes, such as assault, rape, severe injury, and loss of home due to fire, flood, or natural disaster
- A loved one or close friend being victimized by crime
- The unexpected death of a co-worker, whether outside work or in the line of duty
- Witnessing or responding to another person's catastrophe, or simply being at the scene of an accident, assault, suicide, or homicide
- A mass shooting and other incidents of violence inside or outside the workplace

The impact of traumatic stress can severely affect a person's cognitive, emotional, and physical well-being. When distress following a traumatic event continues without support and medical and/or psychological intervention, a person can develop a condition called post-traumatic stress disorder (PTSD). Although PTSD can only be diagnosed and treated by licensed professionals, symptoms can include: mental "flashbacks" or intrusive thoughts about an event; physical illnesses, such as sleep disturbances and appetite changes; and hypervigilance, an oversensitivity to common occurrences (e.g., an extremely startled reaction to a door being shut).[40]

Most communities have access to specialized teams of emergency service workers trained to facilitate an intervention called *critical incident stress debriefing* (CISD), a highly specialized counseling and educational intervention developed by trauma psychologists Jeffrey Mitchell and George Everly, and conducted by a team of trained emergency service and mental health professionals. The purpose of CISD is to help victims or observers of trauma talk about their experiences and feelings in a setting that helps reduce or avoid the likelihood that they might develop PTSD.

In their book *Critical Incident Stress Debriefing*,[41] Mitchell and Everly describe two procedures used in working with those involved in critical stress incidents: debriefing and defusing. A *debriefing* brings together those affected, within 24 to 72 hours of the event, to discuss the incident and learn about community resources available to help them. A *defusing* is a shortened version of a debriefing conducted for a team of workers within a day or two following an incident. Both procedures last about one hour and are facilitated by individuals trained in CISD procedures. (To find out about critical incident stress management professionals or trainings in your area, contact your county Emergency Preparedness Department, local Fire Department, or emergency service provider.)

If a member of your staff is a victim or observer of trauma, suggest that they seek professional support. Even if you're trained as an emergency responder or mental health professional and want to help that staff member, your role as a supervisor could compromise a therapeutic relationship. If a work team has been involved in a trauma, consult with your supervisor or board to determine what community or professional services should be offered.

If you yourself are a victim or observer of trauma, seek appropriate professional support to ensure your continued physical and emotional well-being. No one is invulnerable to the impact of a traumatic event. If you are victimized, reaching out to get the help you need and deserve is a courageous act of self-empowerment and *never* a sign of weakness. You need to take good care of yourself to sustain the physical and emotional stamina you need to do your best work.

Employee assistance programs (EAPs) and community-based services

A staff member may ask you how to access an employee assistance program (EAP), or for a referral to a community service. It's helpful to know in advance about the basic services available through the health insurance plan at your agency. Staff members may be hesitant about seeking professional services, such as mental health counseling or communicable disease testing, because they fear the agency will find out. Even if a staff member doesn't ask, it's helpful to remind them that EAP services are confidential. They're also available to other family members. Workers benefit when their supervisor has basic familiarity with services and opportunities available in the community. Some agencies and communities publish community resource directories that provide up-to-date information about not-for-profit agencies, government assistance programs, and community-based groups.

Workers can also search the Internet for local, state, and national support organizations, but caution must be exercised, because not all websites are reliable sources of information. Web addresses with suffixes such as ".org" indicates a not-for-profit or charitable organization; ".edu" is reserved for accredited educational institutions. These websites are often more trustworthy sources of information than those with domain names ending in ".com," for example, which may sometimes be reliable but are commercial by definition.

A supervisor can collaborate with workers in creating a master resource list for general office use. A master resource list has great potential to be a valuable reference for all workers, both professionally and personally. Agency administrative and clerical support workers are often especially appreciative to have a quick and easy resource guide available to answer general inquiries and help families when a family worker is unavailable.

Many agency leaders receive information from county, state, or federal agencies regarding current trends, demographics, and evaluations of best-practice programs. You may also receive state, regional, and national professional-association newsletters, journals, and program announcements, as well as invitations to events hosted by other agencies. Share them with the appropriate staff members and colleagues, or post them on an electronic bulletin board.

When a supervisor or leader offers to share information that would normally be considered "privileged" or belonging only to management, this is a powerful sign of respect for workers. Leaders often have "blind spots" about their own privilege. When leaders recognize this and, as a result, pass along information more openly, they help workers to have the most complete and accurate information available to help themselves and others.

Resolving conflict

As a leader and supervisor, one of your most challenging and stressful jobs is managing and resolving conflict. Conflict is a state of disagreement or disharmony that can range from mild disagreements to all-out hostility or even war. You can, no doubt, come up with examples of conflicts in your life that were poorly handled; those experiences may have convinced you that all conflict is bad. But conflict can yield positive results if handled with skill and care.

Conflict can be a dynamic force, bringing problems to a head that have long festered beneath the surface. It can keep things moving and force you to look at a situation from another person's point of view. It can even be an expression of caring. Apathy—not conflict—is the opposite of caring. If someone disagrees with you, you can be sure that they care.

There are times when being a supervisor or leader may cause you to feel as if you're the rope used in a game of "tug of war." As a supervisor, you're often pulled in different directions as you try to meet the needs of both families and staff members. As a leader, you're torn between the pressure to achieve results for programs, and the realities of funding limitations and staff capacities. In juggling these competing demands, you can become enmeshed in a submission-aggression loop. *Submission*, in this context, means you do what other people want you to do—or what you think they want you to do—while your own needs are unmet. *Aggression* means that you do whatever gets your needs met, without regard for the needs of others.

You may be caught in a more submissive pattern if you try to:

- Keep everyone satisfied by responding to all their needs all of the time
- Keep everyone's needs at a distance by letting "policies" make the tough decisions for you

Usually, submissive people who put everyone else's desires ahead of their own eventually become resentful and lash out aggressively, or get depressed and withdraw. Aggressive people who get their way at any cost begin to feel quite lonely and swing around to being submissive. It doesn't work well though, because they can't maintain it for very long. So, people go round and round on the submission-aggression loop without communicating clearly or respectfully.

Fortunately, there are more effective and respectful ways to manage and resolve conflict in your organization. In their book *Getting to Yes*,[42] Roger Fisher and William Ury, of the Harvard Negotiation Project, present two approaches to conflict resolution: positional bargaining and principled negotiation.

Positional bargaining reflects the business version of the submission-aggression loop—a negotiation that places greater importance on the content of the agreement than on maintenance of the relationship. The positional bargaining approach involves presenting the best argument by figuring out the other side's deceptions, attacking their weaknesses, and countering their criticisms. You may have observed this approach being used by some of our politicians.

Principled negotiation is a technique that places the highest value on mutual agreement; this approach is highly consistent with the family development model, in four ways:

- A shared guiding principle—that *relationships are as important as outcomes* of a negotiation
- The use of communication techniques to build mutually respectful relationships toward achieving common goals
- The use of facilitation skills to bridge differences that lead to shared decision making
- The use of conflict resolution steps that build toward a "win-win" situation

Here's how principled negotiation integrates the principles of family development practice:

Conditions of Principled Negotiation (Fisher and Ury 1983)	Principles and Practices of Family Development (Forest 1996)
Guiding principle: Separate the people from the problem.	*Guiding principle:* Within every person, there is a bone-deep longing for freedom, self-respect, hope and the chance to make an important contribution to one's family, community and the world.
Communication: Focus on interests, not positions	The Family Development model helps workers learn and practice these skills for communicating with "skill and heart:" • Empathy • Listening well • Mutual respect: assertiveness • Paraphrasing • "I" messages • Factual, emotional, and solution-based feedback • Positive nonverbal communication ("body language")
Facilitation: Invent options for mutual gain	Family development workers learn and practice these techniques: • Planning and organizing meetings that build trust • Brainstorming • Priority setting • Constructive questioning • Summary statements • Handling difficult behaviors
Conflict resolution: Insist on using objective criteria	*Empowerment Skills for Family Workers* presents the following Steps of Conflict Resolution that workers and families can use to get to "win-win" solutions: • Encourage the other person to describe their complaint fully. • Use effective communication skills. • Affirm something that will help the situation. • Look for the need behind the problem. • Together, come up with a list of solutions. • Together, choose one that meets both needs. • Agree on a specific timeline to try out the solution.

Win-win solutions, in which each person's needs get met, require a willingness to satisfy everyone. Not everyone is initially willing to work out such a solution. Some people are so used to looking for a winner and loser in every situation that they think a solution is too "soft" unless they "win" and the other person "loses."

Negotiating using a family development approach

Former FDC Senior Trainer Katie Palmer-House described how her family negotiated the purchase of a small business from their employers, who also happened to be their closest friends. The purchase of the business was complicated, involving the transfer of buildings, inventory, vehicles, and equipment, as well as accounts receivable and funds held in escrow. They had to negotiate an amount to pay the former owners for "good will," or the right to use the name and trademark of the business. They also had to determine and agree upon a radius of miles within which they would agree not to compete. The purchase price of the business was hundreds of thousands of dollars, so they needed to work collaboratively with the former owners, the bank loan officer, and the Small Business Administration to arrange financing within very rigid collateral and guarantee requirements.

The idea of negotiating the purchase of the business seemed difficult enough, but the prospect of endangering their longtime friendship was overwhelming. The process began in "fits and starts": they could bring up the idea in conversation, but when they tried to begin negotiations, the discussion became too intense and seemed to intrude on their relationship. At different times, the terms and conditions of the purchase seemed like a "win-lose" situation for either side. During those times, they would step back from the negotiation efforts to calm down and refocus on the goal, instead of the obstacles.

During meetings, they brainstormed countless ideas to keep progress moving forward, talked about what they thought and felt was needed and why, listened well to each other, put themselves in "their shoes," and developed short-term goals to help break down a monumental task into manageable steps. They never put their friendship on the table as an "issue" up for negotiation. There were compromises made that proved to each of them that the relationship was as important as the outcome of the negotiation.

After a year of negotiation, purchase of the business was finalized and bridged the transition from a respectful employer-employee relationship to a deep and enduring personal friendship. Reflecting on principled negotiation, it was clear that using this approach to bring two sides together in reaching a common goal was a real-life application of the Family Development model. Katie was often skeptical when reading about a new management approach, and wondered if it was as good in reality as it seemed on paper. The process of negotiating the purchase of their business made her realize how truly effective these two approaches can be.

A similar negotiating process might be used when two community agencies with common goals work collaboratively on a grant. Each agency wants the same outcome but must work through many logistics, such as individual roles, budget, and overall commitment. Maintaining a positive relationship is important, because if the grant is funded, they will need to work closely together in the implementation.

Handling blame and criticism

You may wonder: Why is there so much conflict, blame, and criticism? However, these features are a result of living in an adversarial society—one in which a main message is that whenever there's a problem, someone else is to blame and must pay. And everyone does everything they can to make sure it's someone *else* who pays. It's natural for people to want to defend themselves, but reacting defensively can easily lead to continuing blame, criticism, and conflict.

When someone blames or criticizes you, it's hard not to react defensively, and blame and criticize yourself. But defensiveness gets in the way of coming up with a solution that will satisfy everyone's needs. The first step in reaching a solution is to let the person know you understand their complaint; and that doesn't mean you agree with it, necessarily.

Start with communicating effectively through listening, empathy, open-ended questions, and paraphrasing. This will prompt the person to tell you what's on their mind. Next, you can respond with feedback. If the person is angry or upset, use emotional feedback. If the person has a factual complaint, use factual feedback. In the same scenario, an example of factual feedback might be, "I recall your car has been in the shop quite a few times lately." Feedback in which you focus on identifying the resources available is especially helpful. You may have to use several rounds of feedback to understand the person's complaint completely, and it will take great self-control on your part to keep listening to the complaint without immediately defending yourself or retaliating with complaints of your own.

As a supervisor or leader, sometimes you need to address a situation that someone doesn't want to face. Using skills in listening well and "I" messages is a respectful way to do this. For example, let's say one of your workers, who does weekly home visits with families and gets reimbursed by the agency for using his car, begins to have ongoing car repair problems. He begins to fall seriously behind on his work because his car is always in the repair shop. On days when his car is not in the shop, he schedules double the number of his usual home visits to try to catch up on his work. You realize that he might have some financial difficulties that prevent him from buying a newer car, but also that the situation isn't likely to improve until he does. He was hired with the requirement that he had use of a vehicle. Moreover, you know that under these circumstances, he can't work effectively with families. Compare these two examples:

Example without skillful listening and "I" messages:

[Worker]

> It's the agency's fault that my car's in the shop again! If I didn't have to use it more than once a week, I could get by. But every time I get it fixed and use it for work, something else breaks and it's back in the shop!

[Supervisor]

> It's not the agency's fault! You knew when you took the job that using your own car was required! You need to handle this somehow, because it's interfering with you getting your work done in a timely manner!

In the same scenario, if the supervisor were to demonstrate skillful listening, she might say:

> So, you think your car will be in the shop again for the next couple of days? I recall that it was in the shop last week too. It must be frustrating to spend time and money getting the car fixed, and then to have something else break and need repair. I'm concerned, though, that the problems with your car are getting in the way of the work with families that we had planned together. I'm also worried that your car will break down and you'll be stranded somewhere. I realize that these repairs are costing you extra money every week. I know of a free budget-counseling service that helps people figure out ways to afford the things they need. Would you like to have its name and telephone number?

Working effectively with your supervisor, co-leaders, and board

If you are committed to an empowerment approach within your organization, but your own supervisor or board of directors doesn't use this approach with you, you may feel frustrated and misunderstood. A strengths-based approach may be a completely new idea for your organization, or one that has been informally used by just a few members at different levels of the organization. As you learn more about ways to use the family development approach within your organization, it can be disappointing to find that your agency colleagues or professional peers are skeptical, or even openly hostile, to it.

When you consider the investment that your organization has made in time and funding to have you and front-line workers attend FDC training, it can be disheartening to work with people who seem to "talk the talk" but not "walk the walk." Making a paradigm shift takes time. Resist the temptation to make a mental list of those who "get it" and those who don't. We are all growing and changing every day; an individual who's resistant to this paradigm shift could undergo a major transformation next month. Transformations can be triggered by a personal crisis or by an incremental awakening to the value of family development.

Here are some recommendations from an FDC instructor and human service leader who shared how her agency successfully incorporated family development as a philosophy in her organization:

- Time, planning, and building upon the strengths of the organization and staff are the keys to incorporating family development as an organization. Making such a paradigm shift is a slow process; realistically, it can take several years to accomplish.

- To start the process, identify those who believe in the philosophy and develop a committee to develop a vision for incorporating family development in your agency. Using a form such as the Workplace Empowerment Plan can help to identify goals, develop objectives, and plan the steps necessary. The committee should plan to meet periodically to assess progress, identify barriers, and make adjustments to the plan, as needed.

- Outline and document specific ways that using a strengths-based approach can lead to a more effective organization. For example, you could convene a group of workers and families to compile documentation (e.g., job descriptions, intake forms, confidentiality policy, progress forms, performance reviews, monthly or annual reports) that illustrates the strengths and accomplishments achieved through an empowerment approach. Share success stories with other leaders, supervisors, and board members, and demonstrate that you consider them allies in the collaborative work of helping families.

- It takes creativity to think of concrete ways to explain and implement the family development approach in your organization. If agency policies need to change in order to work with families in this way, develop a strong and persuasive case to present to your immediate supervisor or board. Be courteous, appreciative, and persistent. There may be many layers of bureaucracy to work through before the change you desire can take place.

- It's vital that the board of directors, executive director, and key influential leaders of the organization believe and practice a common philosophy. This can be accomplished through presentations and workshops presented by trained committee members or outside sources. Managers and coordinators can be introduced to the philosophy through similar presentations or it can be included as training in management meetings.

- To help staff understand how a family development philosophy will benefit them and the organization, have the committee facilitate activities from the FDC curriculum at staff meetings and other events. It's essential that agency leaders examine (and if necessary, implement changes to) the ways in which the agency's physical environment, policies, and procedures foster staff and family empowerment. This includes tasks such as reviewing the focus of strengths and empowerment within the agency's mission statement, and supporting staff with time, coverage, and needed resources to attend training.

- When collaborative opportunities arise, involve the fiscal officer, program administrators, and executive director in developing service proposals and program initiatives that incorporate a strengths-based approach in setting and achieving outcomes.

- Partners involved in collaborations, whether part of interagency grants or family support programs within the organization, must meet on a regular basis. This includes involving front-line workers in the process of program design, implementation, and assessment. Meetings should be conducted on a regular basis for partners to assess progress, identify barriers, and discuss issues relevant to the collaboration.

- No matter at what level the agency incorporates a family development approach, take the time to acknowledge individual, departmental, and community accomplishments along the way (e.g., in a note, on a certificate, in person, or via other media). Focus on helping a staff member, volunteer, partner agency, or committee identify their strengths and what they've achieved. Acknowledgments and recognition till the "fertile ground" that allows you to reap a future harvest of collaborative outcomes when you sow healthy "seeds" of empowerment along the way.

Managing difficulties with your own supervisor

Your confidence in resolving conflict with a staff member may seem very strong compared with your confidence in managing difficulties with your own supervisor. Discomfort with a power differential can affect any level of working relationship. Just as those you supervise are aware of your power, you're aware of your supervisor's power. Your position may be further complicated if you report directly or indirectly to more than one senior administrator. You may feel "caught in the middle" while trying to manage both relationships.

A helping relationship—whether between a worker and family member, a worker and supervisor, or a supervisor and their immediate supervisor—is based on a set of underlying assumptions and values that shape how that relationship develops. In *The Helping Relationship: Process and Skills*,[43] Lawrence Brammer, at the University of Washington, describes seven personal characteristics of "helpers:"

- Awareness of self and values
- Awareness of cultural experiences
- Ability to analyze the helper's own feelings
- Ability to serve as model and influencer
- Altruism
- Strong sense of ethics
- Responsibility

Relationships present unique opportunities to examine the underlying assumption of your beliefs, attitudes, and values. For example, in the list of characteristics of helpers written above, you may agree that *altruism*—concern for the welfare of others—is a valued shared by many people who work in the helping professions. But how much altruism does it take to be considered altruistic? You may believe that working forty hours each week, attending some after-hours meetings, or occasionally taking work home is evidence enough that you have a high level of concern for the welfare of others. Your supervisor, may however, take work home every night and attend work-related meetings several nights a week. The issue is not about whether you or your supervisor is truly an altruistic person—altruism can be demonstrated in many ways. The issue is how to manage expectations and difficulties if you and your immediate supervisor differ on the underlying assumptions that affect your working relationship.

In *Empowerment Skills for Family Workers*, workers practice using "I" messages as a communication technique that helps express their thoughts and feelings clearly and respectfully. Using "I" messages may feel (and sound) awkward at first, but with practice, you'll be able to express your needs and feelings more naturally in ways that reflect your unique personality.

Here's the basic format for an "I" message:

When _____ happens, I feel
_____, because _____.
I would like _____ to happen.

An "I" message to talk with your supervisor about taking work home to prepare a report for the next morning might look like this:

> When you ask me to have this report in to you first thing tomorrow and it's already 4:30 p.m., it means I have to take work home. I feel frustrated because I have a personal commitment this evening.
>
> I would like to arrange my schedule to work on the report first thing tomorrow and deliver it to you as soon as possible.

There are four typical responses to "I" messages: compliance, resistance, emotions, and statement of needs without acknowledging yours. You can handle these responses to "I" messages in the following ways:

Your Supervisor's Response to Your "I" message	Your Reply
Compliance	gracious acceptance (e.g., "thank you for listening")
Resistance	feedback, listening, responding, and restating your needs
Emotion	give emotional feedback, listening, responding and restating your needs
An expression of their needs	respect their needs, steps to resolve conflict, and commitment to a "win-win" situation

Developing and sustaining a mutually respectful relationship with your supervisor, director, or board may be something you've taken for granted, or considered less important than your relationship with workers and staff members. You may think you have a clear understanding of your supervisor's assumptions about helping relationships. Perhaps you agree with some of them and completely disagree with others. In order to manage expectations and address difficulties with your supervisor, you need to spend time along the way getting to know them and building trust and mutual respect.

If you're having difficulties with your supervisor, reflect on the underlying assumptions you both have about the issue in conflict. Practice using positive "I" messages to find and nurture areas of common ground in your relationship; its quality influences your staff, colleagues, and even your own family members. It's well worth the effort to invest the time, energy, and commitment in making the relationship work effectively for you.

Group dynamics in the workplace

A group is more than a collection of individuals that come together or are united for a common purpose or goal. Group dynamics theory proposes that when a group forms, it becomes a complex system of interrelationships joined through elements such as stages, boundaries, norms, and culture. Whether the group you supervise or lead consists of an entire agency, a department, a unit, or members of a work team, the impact of group dynamics will undoubtedly influence its process at some level. Organizational psychologist Barry Tuckman created a model of group formation and development, and categorized a work group's movement through five different stages[44]:

- *Forming*: a time of orientation, testing boundaries, high group dependence on the facilitator, and high need for structure.
- *Storming*: a period of conflict and resistance as the group struggles with authority, shared commitment, and challenges to the roles of some group members.
- *Norming*: a period during which the group makes a concerted effort to work together and abide by the rules governing group interaction and function.
- *Performing*: a period during which the group's efforts show progress toward reaching outcomes and members can mediate differences to keep the group moving forward.
- *Adjourning*: a time for review, evaluation, leave-taking, and closure.

The ongoing trend to help families and communities find common solutions to resistant social problems through interagency and systems collaboration brings leaders and workers of diverse agencies together. The complex tasks of collaboration, such as joint planning, pooling resources, and evaluating outcomes, require that leaders have up-to-date knowledge and skills in fostering healthy group dynamics.

If you are a supervisor or leader who facilitates an interagency collaboration or work group with members of your own staff, the following table lists some suggestions to help navigate the group dynamics at each stage of development:

During the Stage of:	A Supervisor Can Successfully Manage Group Dynamics by:
Forming	• Helping workers get to know one another formally and informally • Setting mutual expectations and clear boundaries for interaction • Developing policies and procedures for regular feedback and ongoing assessment • Increase group cohesion through activities that allow humor, nonjudgmental sharing, and open discussion
Storming	• Facilitating and mediating ways for workers to manage differing opinions and cultural differences • Providing opportunity to discuss and reflect on the costs and benefits of a program or collaboration for themselves, the organization, and families served
Norming	• Establishing "shared power" norms for members' work duties and overall group outcomes • Sharing relevant information with all group members to sustain the group (i.e. agendas, minutes, meeting summaries)
Performing	• Providing encouragement and reinforcement to the group • Acknowledging individual and group milestones and accomplishments
Adjourning	• Allowing opportunities for the work group to conclude and change roles at the end of the collaboration • Integrating new skills and competencies to regular work

Single- and double-loop learning

Reflecting-in-action is also an effective approach to use for agency goal setting and strategic planning. In their book *Organizational Learning Theory II: Theory, Method and Practice*,[45] Chris Argyris and Donald Schon present two types of organizational learning: single loop and double loop. They argue that organizations "learn" by connecting their values and beliefs with actions to achieve designated goals.

- *Single-loop learning* occurs when organizations act and respond based on a cycle of cause and effect, in which action results in consequences that require new or continued action. This type of learning often results in attempts to solve problems using short-term or "quick fix" solutions.

- In contrast, *double-loop learning* occurs when leaders of the organization reflect and act by recognizing the underlying beliefs and values of the organization, while developing and implementing steps to achieve its goals.

The following graphic illustrates the difference between single-loop and double-loop learning.

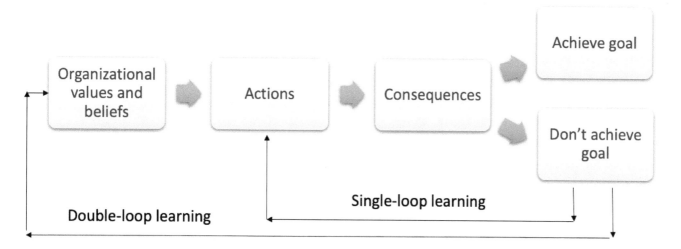

When leaders take time to "reflect-in-action," the results can be both time and cost-effective. Think about the last grant proposal your agency submitted to a funder for a prospective new program. At a time when funders are stressing the importance of developing interagency partnerships that provide comprehensive and "seamless" services and family support, many agencies are eager to collaborate.

In single-loop learning, when an agency receives a funding application or request for proposal (RFP), the following process might happen:

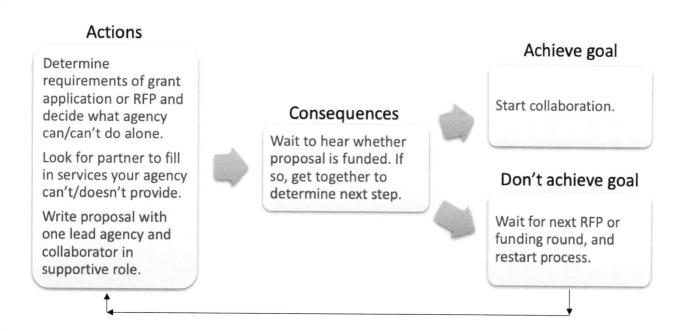

Using double-loop learning (by reflecting-in-action), leaders make decisions about program development according to the guiding principles that underlie the mission and purpose of their organization. In contrast to the previous example, an agency that uses double-loop learning would respond to a grant application or RFP in this way:

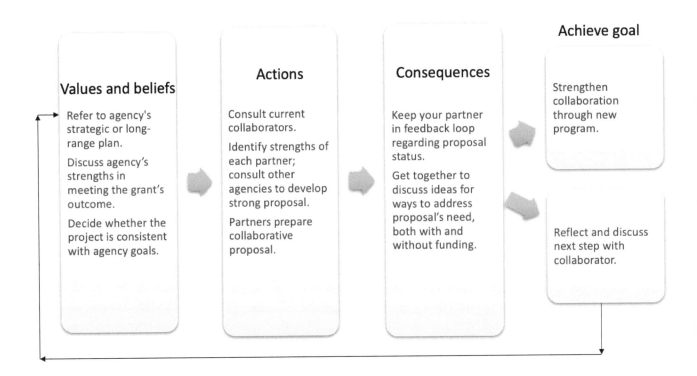

Values and beliefs

Refer to agency's strategic or long-range plan.

Discuss agency's strengths in meeting the grant's outcome.

Decide whether the project is consistent with agency goals.

Actions

Consult current collaborators.

Identify strengths of each partner; consult other agencies to develop strong proposal.

Partners prepare collaborative proposal.

Consequences

Keep your partner in feedback loop regarding proposal status.

Get together to discuss ideas for ways to address proposal's need, both with and without funding.

Achieve goal

Strengthen collaboration through new program.

Reflect and discuss next step with collaborator.

At first glance, "reflecting-in-action" may look like it bogs down the process of program development and decision making in the organization. However, looking more closely, you'll see significant benefits for leaders and organizations:

- Using a strategic or long-range plan (developed in collaboration with staff and board), you'll make better informed decisions about introducing a new program that's consistent with the agency's mission.
- Reflecting-in-action takes external pressure off you to seek out and develop a quick and close working relationship with a new prospective service partner in accordance with a funding opportunity.
- It saves time and resources of preparing grant proposals for new programs your agency isn't yet ready to expand into, or only serves your agency's mission or goal in peripheral ways.
- It strengthens your relationships with existing and new interagency partners, because program development is focused on the agency's strengths and community needs, rather than claims upon territoriality and "turf" issues.

Facilitating effective staff meetings and in-service training programs

As a leader and supervisor, you spend a great deal of time planning, preparing for, and facilitating meetings. Even with technological advances that allow you to email, text, and video-/teleconference, you probably still spend much of your day "on the go," attending meeting after meeting.

In FDC training, instructors use "ice-breakers" and group-forming activities to help participants get acquainted and to re-energize the group during the session. To help you incorporate new and creative ways to facilitate discussion during a staff meeting or in-service training, here are some ideas from *Discussion as a Way of Teaching: Tools and Techniques for Democratic Classrooms*, by Stephen D. Brookfield and Stephen Preskill[46]:

- *Case Study*: Before a staff meeting, ask a volunteer or team to prepare a description of a hypothetical situation, difficulty, or problem the group might face in their work. Distribute the information to staff in advance or provide time for them to read it at the meeting. Facilitate discussion to help the group work collaboratively in identifying steps to resolve the problem.

- *Concept Mapping:* Help the group brainstorm a list of ideas involved in a problem or steps to reach a work outcome. Then ask them to work in small groups to express the ideas or steps in a drawing, diagram, chart, or other schematic (e.g., flowchart, pyramid, circle). In the larger group, ask them to present their ideas. Use a design or combination of designs to work collaboratively on the problem or outcome.

- *Circle of Voices*: This technique is adapted from Native American and First Nations cultures and is designed to give all members an equal opportunity to participate in a period of open but highly structured discussion. Once a topic of discussion has been selected for this activity, members sit around a table and are given up to three minutes each to talk about the topic. The discussion goes around the table, allowing each person to speak without interruption. At the end, discussion can open up, but participants are only allowed to talk about ideas already presented by others in the circle.

- *Circular Response:* As with Circle of Voices, participants have up to three minutes to add their ideas to a structured discussion; but, before adding their own ideas, each participant must first paraphrase the comments offered by the previous person speaking and describe how their comment builds on them.

- *Snowballing*: Discussion begins by hearing participants' responses to a topic, problem, or outcome. Then, the group forms into pairs for a timed discussion. When time is up, the group joins another group for a timed discussion. The groups continue to combine until everyone is reconvened. The facilitator helps process the outcome of the discussion, as well as the process of combining groups.

- *Rotating Small Group Stations*: Introduce the topic for discussion, and post chart paper at different "stations" around the room. Have small groups to work together for a preset time to discuss and record ideas on chart paper at one station. Then, ask each group to move to the next station and develop or build upon the ideas presented. Have all groups visit all stations before the activity concludes.

Using the techniques presented in this chapter for supervising with skill and heart will help you empower yourself and develop increasingly healthy and effective working relationships with your staff members, supervisor, and colleagues. The next chapter, The Inclusive Workplace, explores elements that comprise individual and organizational culture, including some of the common barriers to achieving cultural humility and inclusiveness.

---

[31] The concept of "reflecting-in-action" was developed by Donald Schon.

[32] L. Daloz, *Mentor: Guiding the Journey of Adult Learners* (San Francisco: Jossey-Bass, 1999).

[33] United Way of America. *Measuring Program Outcomes: A Practice Approach.* http://strengtheningfamilies.unitedway.org/evaluating/Sample_LogicModels_A.pdf.

[34] K. Doka, *Disenfranchised Grief: Recognizing Hidden Sorrow* (Lexington, MA: Lexington Books, 1989).

[35] K. Saakvitne and L. Pearlman, *Transforming the Pain: A Workbook on Vicarious Traumatization.* (New York: W.W. Norton, 1996).

[36] N. Schlossberg, E. Water, and J. Goodman, *Counseling Adults in Transition: Linking Practice with Theory.*, 4th ed. (New York: Springer, 2011).

[37] Sheryl Kraft, *Companies are facing an employee burnout crisis* (August 2018), http://www.cnbc.com.

[38] Stress Pulse Survey, EAP Provider Com Psych's first half of 2006. EAP provider Com Psych 2006 Stress Pulse Survey. http://www.stress.org/workplace-stress.

[39] Hyojung Shin, Yang Min Park, Jin Yuan Ying, Boyoung Kim, Hyunkyung Noh, Sang Min Lee, "Relationships between Coping Strategies and Burnout Symptoms: A Meta-analytic Approach," *Professional Psychology: Research and Practice* 45, no. 1 (2014): 44-56.

[40] American Psychiatric Association, "Quick Reference to the Diagnostic Criteria from DSM-111-R" (Washington, DC: APA, 1987).

[41] J. Mitchell and G. Everly, *Critical Incident Stress Debriefing: An Operations Manual* (Ellicott City, MD: Chevron, 1996).

[42] R. Fisher and W. Ury, *Getting to Yes: Negotiating Agreement Without Giving In* (New York: Penguin, 1983).

[43] L. Brammer, *The Helping Relationship: Process and Skills* (Englewood Cliffs, NJ: Prentice-Hall, 1988).

[44] Barry Tuckman developed the first four stages of group development theory in 1965. In 1977, Jensen added the fifth stage of "adjourning" to complete the model as it is presented.

[45] Chris Argyris and Donald Schon, *Organizational Learning II: Theory, Method and Practice* (Reading, MA: Addison-Wesley, 1996).

[46] Stephen D. Brookfield and Stephen Preskill, *Discussion as a Way of Teaching: Tools and Techniques for Democratic Classrooms* (San Francisco: Jossey-Bass, 2005).

Chapter 4—Additional Resources

Books

Argyris, C., and D. Schon. *Organizational Learning II: Theory, Method, and Practice*. Reading, MA: Addison-Wesley, 1996.

Brammer, L. *The Helping Relationship: Process and Skills*. Englewood Cliffs, NJ: Prentice-Hall, 1988.

Daloz, L. *Mentor: Guiding the Journey of Adult Learners*. San Francisco: Jossey-Bass, 1999.

Doka, K. *Disenfranchised Grief: Recognizing Hidden Sorrow*. Lexington, MA: Lexington, 1989.

Fisher, R., and W. Ury. *Getting to Yes: Negotiating Agreement Without Giving In*. New York: Penguin, 1983.

Mitchell, J., and G. Everly. *Critical Incident Stress Debriefing: An Operations Manual*. Ellicott City, MD: Chevron, 1996.

Saakvitne, K., and L. Pearlman. *Transforming the Pain: A Workbook on Vicarious Traumatization*. New York: W.W. Norton, 1996.

Schlossberg, N., E. Water, and J. Goodman. *Counseling Adults in Transition: Linking Practice with Theory*, 4th ed. New York: Springer, 2011.

Turkle, Sherry. *Reclaiming Conversation: The Power of Talk in a Digital Age*. New York: Penguin, 2016.

Articles

Cohen, Esther. "35 Team Building Activities Your Team Will Actually Love." 2019. http://www.workamajig.com/blog/team-building-activities.

Council for Advancement and Support of Education. "4 Conversations Every Leader Needs to Have." *Advancement Weekly* 6 (2017). https://www.case.org/Publications_and_Products/AdvWeeklyJan32017/4_Conversations_Every_Leader_Needs_to_Have.html.

Council for Advancement and Support of Education. "Why Disagreements Can Be Productive." *Advancement Weekly* 6 (2017). https://www.case.org/Publications_and_Products/AdvWeeklyJan32017/Why_Disagreements_Can_Be_Productive.html.

Council for Advancement and Support of Education. "The Cure for low Morale." *Advancement Weekly* 8 (2017). https://www.case.org/Publications_and_Products/AdvWeeklyOctober162017/The_Cure_for_Low_Morale.html.

Goldsmith, Marshall. "Empowering Your Employees to Empower Themselves." *Harvard Business Review*. April 23, 2010. https://hbr.org/2010/04/empowering-your-employees-to-e.

Heathfield, Susan. "The Credo of an Empowering Manager." About.com Guide. 2011. http://www.rdmag.com/article/2011/02/credo-empowering-manager.

Llopis, G. "The 4 Most Effective Ways Leaders Solve Problems." *Forbes* (2013). https://www.forbes.com/sites/glennllopis/2013/11/04/the-4-most-effective-ways-leaders-solve-problems/#571e6bcb4f97.

Ideas for Independent Learning Projects

The following are suggestions for independent learning projects to help you practice or reflect on the principles and practices for supervising with skill and heart. *We encourage you to develop your own independent learning projects that are relevant to your workplace or make modifications to the ones listed below to create a meaningful and manageable plan.*

- Using "bifocal" and "peripheral" vision, write a reflection that describes the characteristics of a work group or committee that you are currently involved with. Then, using Tuckman's theory of group dynamics, describe the stage the group is in right now and how you assessed this. Share ideas about how you, as a facilitator or participant, can help the group advance to the next stage of development or conclude the group in a positive and empowering way.

- Review the assessment forms that your agency currently uses for staff performance reviews. Write a reflection identifying each form's strengths and limitations, using the guidelines for strengths-based assessment presented in this chapter. Generate a list of ways you can collect richer information to complete these forms, ways you can help workers identify goals for use in future assessment, ideas to collaborate on developing assessment criteria, and strategies you would use to create a more strengths-based approach to ongoing assessment with workers.

- Learn about the resources in your community to help workers handle trauma in the workplace. Speak with a county disaster preparedness or emergency services coordinator to find out what training or services are available. Prepare this information and share it with other leaders and supervisors at your agency. Ask for feedback about whether the agency wants to consider offering training or services. If the agency decides to follow up, share information with others who express interest in this area.

- Ask members of one of your current groups, teams, or committees to participate in a brief exercise at an upcoming meeting, using one of the discussion facilitation techniques presented in this chapter. Identify and prepare to facilitate the discussion using the technique of your choice. After you facilitate the discussion, write a reflection on how you prepared to facilitate, how it went, and how the group responded. Compare the quality of ideas and insights using this new technique with those of ideas and insights generated by more traditional discussion techniques.

CHAPTER 5
THE INCLUSIVE WORKPLACE

Learning objectives

- Practice the skills necessary to develop increased cultural humility and inclusiveness in the workplace.
- Understand the benefits and challenges of multiculturalism in a changing American society.
- Explore elements of your personal cultural identity.
- Take steps to strengthen cultural sensitivity and inclusiveness in the workplace.
- Identify aspects of your agency's organizational culture.
- Recognize barriers to achieving multicultural competence and inclusiveness in the workplace.
- Understand how differences in organizational culture may impact collaborative efforts.
- Develop and implement a Leadership Empowerment Plan encompassing the strengths-based principles of family development.

Culture and multiculturalism

Culture refers to a body of human behaviors, customs, beliefs, and social forms that may be found in a distinct, social, racial, religious, geographic, or ethnic group. These behaviors, beliefs, customs, and social forms are embodied in thought, speech, actions, and artifacts, and are dependent on the human capacity for learning and transmitting knowledge to succeeding generations.

Multiculturalism can be defined in two ways[47]:

- A society comprised of, and characterized by, a diversity of cultures
- Acknowledging and promoting coexistence of numerous distinct cultural groups within one nation

The United States has always been a society comprised of a diversity of cultures, beginning with the so-called "melting pot" of largely European immigrants who created a distinctive "American" culture. Today, our society is much more like a salad bowl—broadly multicultural, including individuals and groups representing virtually every culture in the world. Living in a multicultural society brings challenges, as well as opportunities for individual and collective growth and development.

In the book *We Are All Multiculturalists Now*,[48] Harvard sociologist Nathan Glazer defines a *multiculturalist* as a person who:

- Recognizes that personal experience is a bridge from individual cultural identity to its reflection in the larger culture

- Promotes understanding beyond tolerance for other cultures, while building the capacity for respect and personal accountability in restoring the dignity of oppressed and injured cultures

- Acknowledges that a person's multicultural experience results in learning and knowledge that's as valuable as traditional forms of cultural education

- Understands that anti-discrimination programs (e.g., cultural diversity training and affirmative action) are responses to workplace demands for multiculturalism but are not in themselves lasting solutions to the need for multicultural competency

Cultural Competence and Cultural Humility

Cultural competence is the ability to learn from and relate respectfully to people of your own culture, as well as to those of other cultures. It includes adjusting your attitudes and behaviors according to what you learn. Cultural competence is not a skill that, once mastered, remains static; it's a life-long process.

While cultural competence is certainly something to strive for, cultural humility goes beyond cultural competence—when mere knowledge is not enough—delving deeper into self-reflection. *Cultural humility* is having a humble and respectful attitude toward individuals of other cultures that pushes us to challenge our own personal biases, realize we cannot possibly know everything about other cultures, and approach learning about them as a lifelong goal and process.

The concept of cultural humility was first developed by Melanie Tervalon and Murray Garcia in a 1998 academic article published in the *Journal of Health Care for the Poor and Underserved* to be included in training for medical personnel.[49] It has since expanded into the field of social work. Tervalon and Garcia identified three dimensions or facets of cultural humility:

1. *Self-critique is a life-long process.* It's remaining humble and aware of our lack of knowledge about various cultures. More than self-awareness, it requires us to step back to understand our own assumptions, biases and values.[50] Too often, assumptions are made based on generalizations of other cultures.

2. Recognizing and challenging power imbalances for developing respectful partnerships. This is also a key concept of shared power in the family development approach.

3. *Institutional accountability.* Organizations need to model these principles at all levels, from front-line workers to administrators.

Cultural humility aligns well with the family development concept of shared power, in which families are viewed as partners and collaborators in the helping process. Workers learn about the unique cultural experiences of individuals, without the expectation of having to know everything about a specific culture. They learn from communicating with skill and heart, using open-ended questions and reflective listening, working to understand the individual's experience, and any oppression or discrimination that may have shaped it. Workers are open to learning what families have determined is their own personal expression of culture and heritage.

It recognizes that an individual's culture is a rich mix of many influences, experiences, and values, which is why generalizations about a culture don't apply to everyone within that group. On any given day, we may move between several cultures without thinking much about it. For instance, our home/family culture may differ from our workplace culture, social group or religious affiliation. Cultural humility emphasizes that we can't really understand the context of others' lives without being aware and reflective of our *own* background. Mindfulness is a tool to develop cultural humility. It helps us to see things clearly and respond thoughtfully.

How can leaders promote cultural humility in the workplace? Here are a few suggestions[51]:

- Normalize *not knowing*—a willingness to suspend what you know, or what you think you know, about a person from mere generalizations about their culture.
- Utilize or develop assessment tools that give families/individuals an opportunity to share their personal culture to the extent they are comfortable in doing so.
- Facilitate discussion or workshops on cultural self-identification for staff to better understand their own personal culture. (Later in this chapter, we explore this further for leaders.)

This excerpt from the poem "On Caring," by Milton Mayeroff,[52] touches upon cultural competence and cultural humility.

> *To care for another person*
> *I must be able to understand them and their world,*
> *as if I were inside it.*
>
> *I must be able to see, as it were,*
> *with their eyes what their world*
> *is like to them and how they see themselves.*
>
> *I must be able to be with them in their world,*
> *going into their world in order to*
> *sense from inside what life is like for them, what*
> *they are striving to be, and what they require to*
> *grow.*

Cultural humility involves exploring and honoring your own culture, while at the same time learning about and honoring other cultures. It's about cultivating an open attitude and new skills. Developing cultural humility is a lifelong process, one that will, at times, frustrate, confuse, and challenge you; but it will also empower you and deeply enrich your life and relationships. Achieving cultural humility is a life-long journey that begins with *you*.

Cultural identity

Cultural identity refers to an individual's experience of their culture within a historical, social, and environmental context. Many people think "cultural identity" and "ethnic heritage" are synonymous. However, while ethnicity (i.e., racial or national identity) is a central part of a person's cultural identity, there are other equally important elements, such as class, religion, geographic origin, gender, language, age, family form, sexual orientation, body type, and mental skill.

Some elements of cultural identity, such as race or ethnicity, remain the same throughout a person's life. Others, such as family form or religion, are fluid and may change over a person's lifetime.

History and heritage

Each person's unique cultural identity is influenced by their cultural history and heritage. Everyone is affected by the era and social climate in which they live, and by the historical events that take place. Over the past century, individuals and families have no doubt been influenced by the following eras, social movements, and events:

- The Great Depression
- World War II
- The Vietnam War
- The Civil Rights movement
- The Women's movement
- The HIV and AIDS epidemic
- The economic recessions of the 1980s and 2008
- War in the Middle East
- 9/11 and terrorism
- Technology growth including the Internet and social media
- The "Me Too" movement
- Mass shootings and increased gun violence
- The heroin and opioids epidemic
- Climate change and natural disasters

Of course, there are many other significant events and experiences that have shaped our frame of reference. Embedded in an individual's cultural identity is their unique ethnic or cultural heritage. One's ethnic heritage is an inheritance of traditions, customs, stories, and legends passed down from preceding generations.

These "gifts," in the form of age-old wisdom and tradition, help you gain awareness about yourself and those who came before you. Reading the folktales and legends passed down from generation to generation is an entertaining way to understand and appreciate your cultural heritage. Part of your cultural heritage may also include the stories of ancestors (or parents) who came to the United States from other countries. This history includes the relationship with our own culture and with others, including the dominant culture. For example, people may adjust their behavior to fit the dominant culture without giving up their own ways entirely. This process is called *acculturation*. On the other hand, when people choose to adapt to a new culture by taking on that culture's identity and abandoning their own, this is called *assimilation*.

Unfortunately, there have been cases of forced assimilation in the United States, a process that has come to be known as the "melting pot," the idea being that each family's heritage is supposed to "melt" into one "American" culture. Although some people still retain this view, most Americans today embrace the "salad bowl" metaphor, in which everyone's unique cultural heritage is retained, and these distinct cultures are merely mixed together.

Understanding your unique cultural identity

The journey to cultural competence begins with you. By exploring your own cultural identity, you will be better able to understand yourself, learn from others, and develop mutually respectful relationships. As you learned in Chapter 3, you cannot help others to empower themselves if you yourself are not empowered. Likewise, a vital part of becoming culturally sensitive is to become more aware of yourself and your own cultural identity. The question *Who am I?* is one you may have asked yourself many times: "Who am I as a distinct person?" "Who am I in relation to others?" and "Who will I be in the future?" Part of the answers to those questions lies in understanding your cultural background.

Another way to explore the *Who Am I?* question is to repeat it to yourself several times; each time, answer with a deeper interpretation of your previous response. (You could also use this exercise to explore your identity as a leader by asking: Who Am I as a leader?)

A growing understanding of, and pride in, your own cultural background is a strong foundation for expanding your understanding of other cultures. Here are some ways you can become better acquainted with your cultural history and heritage:

- *Talk with family members and others.* Ask questions about your ancestors, relatives, places, immigrations, celebrations, losses, heroes, and heroines. Record what they tell you. Consider researching your genealogy, or at least documenting what the elders in your family know. Ask them to review what you've recorded, and make corrections or additions to make the history more accurate.

- *Visit the important places in your cultural history.* Introduce yourself to people there; tell them that you're exploring your cultural history. Ask for their help.

- *Read about your culture and history.* Realize that what you read (and what you learned in school) might not be accurate. It takes conscious effort to replace misinformation with correct information.

- *Listen to or make the music of your culture.* Enjoy the arts and crafts of your culture, prepare foods, and wear clothes that reflect your cultural heritage. Share these cultural expressions with others. Talk with people you meet along the way. Let them know what you want to learn, and ask them questions in a respectful way.

If you've ever looked through an old album of family photographs, you might have been surprised and amused by the differences in your "look" and your activities over time. The clothes, hairstyles, and things you may chuckle over from the past were expressions of your cultural identity at that time. Are those same things important to you today?

For most people, some aspects of cultural identity evolve over time, while others remain constant throughout life. Identifying and understanding your own cultural identity development is an evolving process of self-discovery and the first leg of the journey to cultural competence.

Respecting and valuing all cultural backgrounds

It's natural to feel most comfortable interacting with people who are like you; however, as a supervisor or leader, you will likely be working with people who are very different from you. For example, you may have a colleague who, like you, has similar ethnicity, age, and educational background. Yet, they may be unmarried and involved in a weekend sports league, while you're married with children and spend your Sundays attending church. Or, you may have a Hispanic colleague who's much younger, but with whom you spend many weekends sharing your common passion for scrapbooking.

You are a culturally rich person with your own blend of traits, experiences, and knowledge. If you were to describe yourself in each of the areas listed below to a close friend, what would you say?

- race
- ethnic background
- language
- gender
- sexual orientation
- class (e.g., poor, working class, middle class, wealthy)
- family form
- age
- spirituality
- geographic identity

- body type
- mental skill

Now, imagine that you are not describing yourself to a close friend, but to someone who has the power to say "yes" or "no" to hiring you or the power to evaluate your work and grant you a raise or promotion. How would you describe yourself? Are there aspects of your cultural identity that you would leave out in order to "fit" with what you think is more acceptable? If you had to do that repeatedly, what would happen to those aspects of your identity? How would it feel to believe that you had to hide parts of yourself?

As a supervisor or leader today, you will increasingly be working with people from diverse cultural groups in your agency and in your community. While it's not possible to learn everything about each of the cultures you encounter, it is possible for you to expand your understanding by:

- Exploring your own culture and examining your values and beliefs
- Knowing what cultural competence and cultural humility are, and why it is vital for leaders and supervisors
- Approaching each worker's culture respectfully
- Finding reliable sources of information about a culture
- Developing the skills needed to learn from and work with cultures different than yours
- Becoming more comfortable with not always knowing how to behave with people from diverse cultures, and making honest mistakes during your lifelong learning process

It's easy to communicate with another person who shares your own cultural background. But what if there are real cultural differences? Here are some categories of behavior that may affect you or staff member's understanding and sensitivity to other cultures:

- Use and meaning of eye contact and touch
- Interpretation of what level of "personal space" is comfortable or intrusive
- Varied levels of literacy in reading, speaking, and writing skills, in and between family members
- Tolerance of and comfort with silence
- Approach when speaking with elders and those in authority
- Orientation to time in attending meetings or appointments
- Gift-giving and appropriate ways to express feelings of gratitude
- Customs regarding which family members may speak to others about family matters
- Open expressions of emotions, especially disappointment, anger, grief, and fear
- Rights of parents, spouses, and others to making important decisions about children, about another spouse, or about aging, dependent parents
- Offering of assistance to someone who's differently abled, in physical, social, or developmental ways
- Approaches to negotiating agreements

Simply asking a person for more information or advice when approaching a discussion or interaction is the most direct and considerate way to show respect for individual cultural differences. It can be frustrating at times to think that communicating well with people from different cultures takes a lot of time and attention. You may feel like a stranger in your own community! But the reality is, our collective culture continues to evolve every day, and clinging to the ideal of a static "American" culture can only limit everyone's ability to develop rewarding relationships with others. While there will always be some characteristics and behaviors more highly valued and rewarded in this society, every time you demonstrate and affirm that diversity is also a value worth promoting and celebrating as part of our universal "human" culture, you're also showing respect for other cultures.

Much of what is generally known about other cultures is inaccurate and often not based on authentic personal contact. How have you learned about other cultures? How do you learn about other cultures now? You've probably learned from a variety of sources over your lifetime, such as TV, radio, newspapers, social media, magazines, movies, songs, advertising, school experiences, textbooks, your family, friends, co-workers, and community. But what have you actually learned? Perhaps a blend of stereotypes, misinformation, and accurate information.

As a family support professional, you usually interact with the most troubled families in a community. The families who come to your offices are often the most vulnerable of their cultural group. It's not surprising that you may have developed opinions about an entire group from your experiences with some families. As you strive to learn more about different cultures, it's important to be cautious about making sweeping generalizations about or between cultural groups.

To expand your cultural awareness and competence, you need to know strong, healthy people within a cultural group. Political, educational, and religious leaders in a community usually recognize the value of educated agency workers and are generous in providing accurate information. You can begin to cultivate relationships with leaders from other community groups if you want to learn more about a particular community issue. Consider volunteering to serve on a task force or local committee that addresses areas of personal interest to you or your agency. Some organizations conduct periodic community- or agency-based needs assessments and arrange to meet with school superintendents, judges, probation department administrators, and clergy, as well as locally elected officials. These people can provide valuable insight and knowledge about the culture(s) in your community, and the needs and concerns of all residents.

The multigenerational workplace

Another aspect of culture and inclusiveness is the presence of multiple generations in the workplace. Perhaps more than at any other time in history, it's not unusual today to have four different generations of workers within an organization: the "Silent Generation" (also called "Traditionalists"), "Baby Boomers," "Generation X" (also "Gen X"), "Millennials," and the latest, "Generation Z" (also "Gen Z" or "iGen"). According to Pew research, Millennials surpassed Gen X'ers in 2015 as the largest generational cohort in the workplace.[53] While there has been some debate over the accuracy of these categories, as a rule:

- Silent Generation: born before 1946
- Baby Boomers: born 1946–1964
- Gen X: born 1965–1980
- Millennials: born 1981–1996
- Gen Z: born after 1996

While there are clearly differences in the ways each generation sees the world, based on their life experiences, research scientist Jennifer Deal, with the Center for Creative Leadership, found that all generations of working age value the same things.[54] Deal says that negative stereotypes for each generation have helped to create a myth of generational differences in the workplace. For instance, Millennials, as an example, seem to be getting an especially bad rap these days. Deal's research found these commonalities among generations:

- Everyone wants respect, though it may be perceived differently among generations. For example, older generations may want their opinions to be given the weight they deserve, while younger generations may want leaders just to pay attention and listen to what they have to say.

- Leaders must be trustworthy. Trust develops over time when leaders follow their words with action and support staff, along with keeping sensitive information confidential.

- Nobody likes the prospect of change. Resistance to change has little to do with age but more to do with how much one stands to gain or lose.

- Loyalty depends on context. The level of effort and number of hours worked has more to do with a staff member's position and level within the organization than with age. This might help to explain why some lower-paying or lower-level positions tend to have greater turnover.

- Everyone wants to learn and ensure they have the training to do their job well.

- Everyone likes feedback, though each person is unique in how they may want that feedback, for example, verbal feedback versus an electronic message.

Here are some strategies for leaders to successfully work across generations[55]:

- Establish respect. Consider what motivates people, what experiences they might have had and what their working styles are.

- Be flexible and accommodating. Differences in generations are often related to their stage of life rather than age. For example, an increasing number of Gen Xers are facing responsibilities caring for elders as well as children. This is sometimes called the "sandwich generation" and was previously more commonly coined for Baby Boomers.

- Avoid stereotyping. There are many charts listing both the positive and negative characteristics of each generation. While there are certainly some elements of truth to this, such as younger generations growing up with and being skilled at technology, keep in mind that everyone is unique.

- Learn from one another. Each generation has a wealth of knowledge and experience to share. Focusing on individual strengths rather than generational differences will foster an inclusive workplace across the ages.

Barriers to achieving cultural competence and cultural humility

Many people welcome the reality of living in a multicultural society and embrace the opportunity to enhance their cultural competence. Others, especially those used to being in privileged positions, are angry about giving up that privilege and having to pay some of the costs of an increasingly diverse society. They're afraid of change and may go to great lengths to avoid confronting their own ignorance and bigotry.

Resistance to the openness and tolerance required to live in a multicultural society results in four types of barriers to cultural competence: privilege, prejudice, discrimination, and oppression.

- Some people, who enjoy privileged status through membership in a certain social or ethnic group, are resistant to change and believe they are entitled to *privilege* because of their social or economic position. They have blind spots about their privilege, believing it's the result of their own hard work or superior intelligence.

- People view others through the lens of their cultural background and experience. *Prejudice* occurs when opinions and judgments about a person or group are formed without knowledge or examination of the facts. Treating someone from a cultural group as representative of that group or an expert on that culture can also be an act of prejudice. Prejudice is the expression of ignorance and intolerance, and can result in irrational hatred, even violence.

- *Discrimination* occurs when a person, group, or organization acts on their prejudices. For example, if someone has negative opinions about transgender individuals based on incorrect information or personal bias, that's prejudice. If the same person is an employer who, without regard for individual qualifications, refuses to hire a transgender person, that's discrimination. While prejudice causes conflict between people of different cultures, institutional discrimination causes perhaps the most harm in our country. There are laws prohibiting some forms of discrimination. Federal law protects people from job discrimination based on sex, national origin, religion, abilities, and age. In addition to federal laws, some states and communities have anti-discrimination statutes, for example, housing discrimination based on sexual orientation. It's important to know the laws in your community. Systematic (i.e., embedded in the system) discrimination against certain groups in society may result in oppression (see below). A person can do "everything right" and still face discrimination and oppression because of their color, age, gender, or religion.

- *Oppression* occurs when power and authority are used to persecute or subjugate individuals or groups. It's intentional force, grounded in prejudice and hatred, that inflicts great pain and suffering. Oppression takes the act of discrimination to a dangerous and harmful level.

Racism, sexism, classism, and ageism are all forms of discrimination that can result in oppression. Other conditions or life circumstances vulnerable to discrimination or oppression are:

- country of origin, "poor English," or immigrant status
- religion
- size or appearance (e.g., being labelled "fat," "short," "ugly")
- lack of formal education
- physical disability
- being lesbian, gay, bisexual or transgender
- having a chronic illness
- current or prior history of substance abuse
- felony conviction or prison record

Racism and other "isms" based on gender, financial status, or age are the result of prejudicial beliefs and acts of discrimination upheld by power. Oppression can be experienced by people for many reasons, and some people are victims of multiple forms of oppression.

It's never useful to compare oppression—to argue that one is worse than another, or that combating or eliminating one kind of oppression is more important than eliminating others. It helps to compare societal oppression to a bicycle wheel, with racism, sexism, and other "isms" as spokes on the wheel. Whatever can be done to remove or weaken one spoke could help reduce the damaging effects of societal oppression, which serve to reinforce acts of power and privilege at the expense of others. The goal is to create a society in which *every* person is entitled to respect and has access to needed resources.

The fundamental mission of most educational institutions and family support organizations is to counteract the hardships and negative impacts that these barriers impose on individuals and families. The quality and success of relationships with families reflect the extent to which workers have developed their own cultural competence and cultural humility, and the extent to which their organization supports it. Family support organizations may "talk the talk" by writing mission statements and setting guidelines that address the need to reduce and eliminate these barriers. But when organizations support their workers in developing cultural competence and humility, they truly "walk the walk" in helping families achieve their goals in accordance with the principles of family development.

Your agency's "organizational culture"

Just as there are many different aspects to an individual's culture, the same is true for organizations. They could range from the diversity of staff members to how comfortable people feel when they come to an agency seeking services. In *Organizational Culture and Leadership*,[56] organizational psychologist Edgar Schein writes that "organizational culture" is comprised of the following components:

- Norms (unspoken rules and habits governing workplace interactions)
- Values
- Habits of thinking
- Customs
- Climate
- Philosophy
- Symbols

In carrying out the mission of an organization, leaders, staff members, and the people they serve interact with each other according to a set of unspoken and accepted beliefs or assumptions. For example, an assumption we might make about family support organizations (and generalize to their leaders and workers) is that they operate according to the principle that all people have the right to respect and dignity, regardless of life circumstance. When families approach a family support agency and are treated poorly, they may be confused and angry because this unspoken assumption (that they'd be treated with respect) was proven wrong. Over time, if that assumption is proven invalid through continued interactions with the agency or its staff members, it's reasonable to see how families might lose faith in their ability to get help from family support agencies.

To clarify the less obvious aspects of your agency's organizational culture, read the following four statements, and place an "X" on the continuum to indicate where you think the culture of your agency is focused right now. For example, if you place it on the center line, that indicates you believe your agency is equally focused on "individual responsibility" and "team-oriented accountability." If you place it to the left of the center line, that indicates you believe your agency, to a greater or lesser degree, is focused on "individual responsibility."

Basic Elements of Organizational Culture

Statement 1) My organization is currently focused on staff members acting with:

◆────────────────────────────┼────────────────────────────◆

individual responsibility   *team-oriented accountability*

Statement 2) Staff members in my organization feel the agency:

◆────────────────────────────┼────────────────────────────◆

promotes personal and   *deters personal and*
career development   *career development*

Statement 3) My organization's services and programs are currently offered to the community:

◆────────────────────────────┼────────────────────────────◆

independently   *collaboratively*

Statement 4) Most staff members believe my agency to be:

◆────────────────────────────┼────────────────────────────◆

paternalistic or   *entrepreneurial*
maternalistic

Next, write a description of your response to each of the statements above: (For example, "My organization is currently focused on members acting with a great deal of team-oriented accountability.")

Organizational Cultural Assessment

1) My organization currently focuses on members acting with

_____
(fill in your response to statement #1)

2) Staff members in my organization feel the agency

_____
(fill in your response to statement #2)

3) My organization's services and programs are currently offered to the community

_____
(fill in response to statement #3)

4) Most staff members believe our organization to be

_____
(fill in your response to statement #4)

The statements you've just completed are *your* assessment of aspects of the structure, nature of relationships, community perception, and image of your organization. The next step is to learn from other leaders and staff members, as well as key advisors and community stakeholders, whether these are shared beliefs and perceptions. For now, just focus on exploring the explicit and implicit assumptions about your organization without thinking about changing the culture. Here are some ideas to consider in developing a clear picture of your agency's current organizational culture:

- Identify the "cultural brokers" among workers and staff members who help your agency develop multicultural competence with families, service partners, and the community.
- Which agencies are your organization's natural allies? Which are the most challenging to work with?
- How would you describe their organizational cultures?
- In what ways do your organization's cultural assumptions promote or hinder the ability to work with existing and new collaborators?

Later in this chapter, you'll learn about ways to introduce and facilitate cultural change in your organization, using principles of the family development model.

Organizational cultural competence and inclusiveness

Leaders and staff members like to see their agency's programs as unique and distinctive from all others, even from those agencies who offer nearly identical programs. Sometimes, but not always, an agency's name sufficiently describes its program and services. Yet its name, motto, location, and even its most recognized program may not be indicative of its organizational origins, identity, and focus. Helping organizations can be community-sponsored, government-supported, faith-based, not-for-profit, affiliated with for-profit companies, nationally known, or neighborhood-based, just to name a few possibilities. Supervisors and leaders may have become qualified for their position because they've earned professional degrees, completed specialized training, or passed a civil service exam; or they may simply be selected for promotion.

An organization's culture is created through a combination of thoughts, feelings, attitudes, beliefs, values, and behavior patterns shared by its members. In *Organizational Theory II: Theory, Method and Practice*, Chris Argyris and Donald Schon define *organizational culture* as a continual process of growth as organizations adapt to internal and external pressures and their leaders promote, shape and manage change.[57]

Organizational cultural competence is the collective ability of leaders and staff to learn from and relate respectfully to those from other personal and organizational cultures. Although cultural competence and cultural humility are generally seen as a primary task for those who work most directly with families, those who supervise and lead organizations—including the organizations themselves—are also responsible for the delivery of culturally competent services. And, just as one cultural group is part of a multicultural society, an individual family support organization is part of a large family support-system culture. A culturally competent organization is one that allocates resources, sets specific goals, and develops policies that support the agency and staff members in working with cultural differences in the population(s) they serve.

Cultural competence in an organization means:

- Recognizing the strengths in all cultures
- Respecting cultural differences
- Using cultural knowledge to design and provide services

Barriers to an organization's cultural competence

In many ways, organizations reflect the similar dynamics of relationships that occur in our own families and in the larger culture. The barriers of privilege, prejudice, discrimination, and oppression that occur in society can also be found in workplace culture.

1. Workplace privilege

At times, supervisors and leaders are "nearsighted" with regard to how their position of privilege is viewed by workers and staff. For example, if a supervisor makes a decision that a worker doesn't agree to but must comply with, that worker may feel their supervisor exercised their privilege in that situation. When a leader takes time off during working hours to compensate for work done on evenings or weekends, it can also be seen by other workers as an act of privilege, especially if others are not able to do the same.

2. Workplace prejudice

Many supervisors and leaders are selected or promoted to manage and lead in organizations because of their sensitivity, respect, and ability to work with people of diverse cultures. Yet, upon becoming a supervisor and leader, that same individual can become isolated and insulated from their ability to interact with, and relate to, workers as individuals. The constant demands and pressures of leadership can result in the need to make decisions or implement new policies or procedures from past experiences, intuition, or limited information. In the heat of a situation affecting a few workers, a leader or supervisor may prejudge that all workers have similar concerns, needs, or difficulties.

Even with the best of intentions, a leader's decision to take action intended to correct a situation involving a few workers may result in potential inconvenience for other workers. For example, a leader may believe that some workers need to improve their technology skills. There is funding available to provide training for these workers, as well as some additional funding to train the rest of the staff. Deciding whether to send some or all staff to training requires judgment based on having adequate information. If the leader isn't able or willing to gather full information on the need for technology training, it's likely that they'll make a prejudicial decision.

Many people hold strong religious or personal beliefs that affect their attitudes toward individual lifestyle choices, sexual orientation, medical issues, different abilities, and other aspects of contemporary culture. However, for supervisors and leaders, the question must be—given that some people are gay, lesbian, bisexual, transgender, HIV-infected, or non-English speaking—how are you going to treat them? Can you set aside your prejudices and treat these individuals fairly? And can you create a safe and respectful working environment? Because of extreme prejudice in some areas, many individuals are afraid to discuss personal details of their lives. For example, a worker or colleague you know may have a parent, child, or partner who has HIV. A worker who is single and living with a same-sex roommate may be lesbian or gay. Affirming, rather than prejudging, the reality of people's lives and loves will make you a more effective supervisor and leader.

3. Workplace discrimination

Discrimination can occur on personal and institutional levels. If you refuse to shop in a store because the owner is a member of a certain cultural group, that's an act of personal discrimination. If your agency hires a less-qualified person over a well-qualified one with a disability, that decision is an act of institutional discrimination.

Cultural sensitivity training is one type of program used to bring more conscious awareness of the need to value and support diversity in organizations. Yet, if sensitivity training is offered by an agency as a "mandatory in-service," or as an attempt to defuse an already inflammatory situation, the intended benefits will be negligible. Job seekers and employees have some protection from overt institutional discrimination through equal opportunity employment and anti-discrimination laws and policies. However, more covert forms of discrimination can go unchecked and become insidious, infectious acts of institutional discrimination.

To avoid letting covert forms of discrimination become a part of the institutionalized pattern of behavior, leaders and supervisors need to provide regular opportunities for staff to develop cultural sensitivity by taking these proactive steps:

- Communicate regularly with staff about respecting cultural differences at work, with families, and with each other.
- Be a role model who recognizes strengths in all cultures.
- Use cultural knowledge to design and implement programs for use both within your agency and in your agency's work with families.

4. Workplace oppression

One form of oppression sometimes found in organizations is termed the "glass ceiling" effect: systematic discrimination against individuals in less-powerful minorities attempting to advance to higher positions, which serves as an "invisible" barrier to such advancement. This type of institutionalized oppression can happen in small community-based organizations, as well as multinational corporations. Individuals in this situation can be treated as a "minority," even if they're actually a member of a majority group.

According to the U.S. Department of Labor, women comprised nearly 57% of the labor force in 2016. Census reports indicate that the number of women in the workforce has steadily risen over the past few decades. Yet despite this evidence, the earning gap between men and women in the United States persists. In 2014, women who worked full time, year round, earned an average of 79 cents for every dollar earned by men; this wage gap has remained consistent into 2019.[58] Women are also vulnerable to the glass ceiling effect and are underrepresented in STEM (science, technology, engineering, and math) occupations, which tend to be higher paying.

Another insidious and incapacitating form of workplace oppression is *internalized* oppression, in which an individual comes to believe that acts of oppression against them are justified. When a person is promoted to supervising staff who were previously their co-workers, the one promoted may be criticized for "selling out" or trying to be better than the others. While they may be pleased to have been promoted, they may feel extremely torn, knowing that ultimately their strongest source of support will come from being respected within the groups they supervise. Even if they actively sought this opportunity for advancement, they may begin to question their own ability to do the job effectively and thus internalize the criticism received from former workplace "friends." The person promoted may even come to believe they were promoted merely as a "token" used by leaders for their own ends. While this situation can be uncomfortable at first and require that both the new supervisor and former co-workers redefine their workplace roles, it doesn't have to remain contentious.

If you've personally experienced this type of situation, you know there are no easy answers. If a colleague or co-worker is having a similar experience, the most important thing you can do is to help them look at the choices they face. If you're an agency leader who's promoted a worker or staff member to be supervisor of a group, you can help by instituting practices in the organization that ensure equitable access to advancement, based on measurable milestones of effective work performance.

Clashes between organizational and family cultures

A major benefit for organizations that encourage cultural competence is that staff members are more aware of the impact of their own cultural identity on families. Workers realize that, for example, eligibility requirements are just the starting point in a family's goals of healthy self-reliance. When workers offer families interagency referrals in seeking specialized services, they do it not simply to "close a case," but because they've developed relationships of mutual respect with those families.

Workers are often in a "no-win" position when their agency's procedures conflict with the values and customs of a family's culture. In American society, it's customary that family workers speak directly with as many family members as possible to learn about a family's strengths and concerns. If a family member is unwilling or reluctant to speak directly with a worker to avoid dishonoring family cultural customs, the worker will be torn between trying to offer respectful assistance and having to abide by the agency's policy of family participation. Even if this early obstacle is overcome, conflict may arise again if the requirements for agency services are tied to actions that disregard or disrespect a family's cultural customs.

The Spirit Catches You and You Fall Down is an excellent book by Anne Fadiman that portrays the real-life, tragic cost of a clash between a Hmong family and an organizational culture.[59] Shortly after birth, Lia Lee, an infant whose family came to California as refugees in the 1980s, was diagnosed as suffering from life-threatening grand mal epileptic seizures. Her Hmong parents believed her condition to be a sign of shamanic and mystical power, and treated her seizures in ways that Western doctors could neither understand nor medically condone. The story chronicles the first four years of Lia's life, seen through the eyes of her parents, doctors, nurses, social workers, foster parents, and others, all of whom felt their efforts would save her life. The heartrending lesson behind the story is that there are no simple answers when the clash between family and organizational cultures affects life-and-death situations.

Another example is the measles epidemic of 2019. While science has proven the vaccine for measles is safe and effective, there are still families who refuse to vaccinate their children because it goes against their religious or personal beliefs, thus placing those with compromised immune systems in jeopardy.

Fortunately, most clashes between family and organizational cultures don't end in tragedy. However, ignoring the clash or pretending it doesn't exist can lead to serious problems. Workers and families know that clashes exist, and they rely on supervisors and leaders to provide guidance in negotiating conflict in respectful ways. Leaders must be willing to explore and correct underlying assumptions in their organizational culture when those assumptions collide with the best interests of a family's healthy self-reliance.

Developing an inclusive organization

Effective outreach and networking are the first steps in building relationships beyond your own agency. Looking for similarities in philosophy or practice in other agencies and asking for information to share with your staff are good places to start.

Another way is to cultivate relationships with leaders of other family support organizations that may lead to future interagency collaborations. How do you reach out to other agencies? Supervisors and leaders need to know how to do so in creative, effective ways that benefit from family development opportunities. Agencies can increase their ability to work effectively with other agencies in four ways:

- Be responsive to inquiries and referrals from other agencies.
- Make sure other agencies understand and support the programs and services your agency offers.
- Welcome other agencies that show interest in your program.
- Strive to build and maintain mutually respectful relationships.

Many helping organizations have been quite passive about their outreach. They've shared information about a new or existing program, then waited for a response from families or other agencies. This approach has changed recently. Today, human service agencies are increasingly using marketing techniques such as focus groups to get *input from the people who actually use their services.* To be successful, agencies need to know what products or services their "clients" need and want.

Offering referrals to other services and helping families referred by other agencies are among the most valuable services you can provide. Unless families have been involved with many agencies over a period of years, they usually aren't aware that agencies have "turf" or other territorial issues.

Develop mechanisms for ongoing communication within existing interagency collaborations that prevent or address turf issues and territoriality. An agency leader at a leadership focus group shared this perspective on turf issues and collaboration:

> *Supervisors need to learn the strengths-based approach is important with other agencies as well as with families. If that agency has a strength, then we need to collaborate and not let this, 'That's my territory' thing come into play.*

> *There are lots of different politics between agencies, territories, and mandates. Agencies often go to the same funding sources. If one agency was denied something, another agency (in the same community) gained it. Then two days later, we're sitting together looking to collaborate and having to negotiate all those feelings.*

Territoriality and turf issues that arise between organizations often occur as a reaction to external factors. Political pressure and current social trends may fix attention onto a "new" issue and, to accommodate the demands of taxpayers or special interest groups, funders may decide to "divide the pot" by giving less money to long-established programs. It would be naïve to think that leaders can resolve these issues simply by deciding not to feel threatened. But you can avoid many turf issues and be well-positioned to handle those that arise by doing the following:

- Focusing on building the strengths of your staff members, colleagues, and agency's programs and services. When it's a choice between spending your time in turf battles or doing great work, turf battles are seldom the better choice.

- Acknowledging and appreciating the strengths of collaborators for their unique contributions to families. Be gracious. You may have to put extra effort into keeping your partner in the communication-feedback loop, as many interagency collaborators are very busy with a variety of projects, or are handling pressing concerns in their own agencies.

- Acting responsibly in ways that serve the best interests of families and the greater community. When issues arise that have potential to create defensiveness or threats between agencies, express your concerns privately. Your integrity is worth more than this one turf issue.

Here are some other recommendations:

1. *Encourage workers to participate in local human service councils, and to attend regional family support meetings.* Ask the workers to take notes and prepare a brief summary to share with supervisors and other workers. Sharing responsibility for outreach and networking among leaders, supervisors, and family workers benefits the entire organization in two important ways: a worker feels trusted to represent the organization in a positive way, and other organizations recognize that your agency values the abilities of front-line workers.

2. *Help your organization improve its access to computer, information management, and communication technology.* While some organizations provide staff with laptops and cell phones, there is no set agency standard in this area. Individual programs or agency centers may even have different access to technology. Consider situations that might point to your organization's need for better technology, for example:

- Workers make home visits (sometimes during evenings and weekends) and must use their personal cell phones to contact families or get help in an emergency.

- Budgets or reports are delayed because staff members don't have the most up-to-date computer software or training to do their work efficiently.

- Answering the telephone takes away from time staff members need to complete necessary paperwork or work with families. Improving access to technology is a sound investment for your organization, even if this must be done gradually.

3. *Interagency training (e.g., FDC) is a powerful tool for networking with other agencies.* When staff members from several different agencies participate in the same training, they get to know each other and become familiar with the services other agencies offer. They also begin to speak the same language and use the same approach in working with families.

An agency director who earned the FDC credential shared this perspective on FDC interagency training:

"I've taken a lot of supervisory training, but I really haven't taken to any like I've taken to the Family Development curriculum. Usually in supervisory trainings, all you have are supervisory people, all thinking one way. A lot of times we've sat in a training thinking that we were the 'experts' and wondering what can we learn from this trainer. Family Development training was just so much different. Our training program had people from different agencies, people with degrees, people with no degrees, just a whole different dynamic. The strength of Family Development training is the diversity. The training program has had input from across the line, and that's what really makes it viable."

Supervisors and leaders limit their ability to try new ideas when they fail to think "outside the box"—in creative and innovative ways—and when the only opinions and perspectives they hear are those of their peers. The willingness to trust the perceptions of those closest to a situation, such as family workers and families, is demonstrating inclusiveness. Interagency training for supervisors and leaders provides helpful feedback on how you perceive yourself, and how others perceive you. It also provides a discreet opportunity to observe other agencies with whom you might collaborate in the future.

Interagency collaboration

In recent years, funders have emphasized the value of interagency collaboration because they can achieve more substantial results with collective efforts. Collaboration can vary from a short-term project, such as co-sponsoring of a training workshop, to a longer-term initiative effort, such as a task force to develop new services needed in the community. Interagency collaborations can begin when agencies make decisions together to study issues, set goals, and even apply for funding of new services and programs.

In *Empowerment Skills for Family Workers*, workers learn three ways that agencies typically work together to achieve goals:

1. *Coordination*: sharing information about services, making referrals, or listing another agency's events in brochures or newsletters.

2. *Cooperation*: agreeing to help each other out in specific ways, such as working together to provide different services to the same family.

3. *Collaboration*: agreeing to work on a common goal that is beyond what each partner can accomplish alone. Collaboration involves joint planning, pooling resources, and evaluating the outcomes together. Partners in a collaboration usually need to make some changes in the ways they work.

There are many ways to collaborate with other agencies. The primary type of interagency collaboration is between front-line workers and an individual or family with multiple needs. Few agencies can meet all the service needs of families, so they *must* collaborate. For example, a family conference is a family-run, decision-making meeting that can include workers from one or more agencies. Workers from different agencies may be asked to participate in a family conference to support the family or to take an active role in helping to bridge gaps in services.

Another type of interagency collaboration occurs when agencies formally decide to connect their services in ways that provide better support for families. Sometimes agencies feel limited in the amount of collaborative work they can do because their funding does not value collaborative efforts.

Most helping organizations are part of larger human service systems. The capacity of workers or agencies to work together can be limited, unless the systems they're part of recognize the value of collaboration. Organizations may receive support from a state or federal government agency, and if that agency doesn't value collaboration, the local organization's ability to devote resources to collaborative projects may be restricted.

The most effective systems-level collaboration begins with needs assessment to determine whether it even makes sense to work together. Too often, systems begin to collaborate simply because someone has an idea for a program that requires several partners, or because funders require interagency collaboration. Worthwhile initiatives for families can emerge from these types of collaborations, but it's more effective to begin with collaborative assessment of the community and use it as a springboard to developing services the community really *needs*. Families need to be given a major voice in this process. They often have very different perspectives on the community's problems and, especially, the solutions to those problems.

Interagency collaboration is seldom simple and is often one of the most challenging aspects of leadership. Despite the challenge of collaboration, there are many benefits. Collaboration between workers and families makes it possible for families to reach their goals. Interagency collaborations can enhance an organization's multicultural competence and accomplish much more than one agency can accomplish alone. Helping systems can develop networks that create "seamless" transitions between services for families.

Collaboration can make more efficient use of resources, thereby saving money and time. It can bring additional creative energy and increased resources to solve a problem. Collaboration can also promote large-scale reorientation to the family development approach, because as leaders, workers, agencies and systems collaborate, they learn and share new ways of working with families.

A supervisor at a leadership focus group said:

> *You might go into collaboration where you are not going to get much funding, but you might get some visibility, and that may be what your agency needs then. In another situation, you might get funding, but then you need to be aware that the other collaborators may need visibility.*

Collaborations work best when partners are aware of, and responsive to, each other's needs. Collaboration often breaks down when one or more partners set goals and then expect the other "collaborators" to support these goals. This does not mean that everyone must make every decision together. It does mean, however, that collaborators must decide together who will be in on what kinds of decisions. Sometimes, collaborations deteriorate and fail because people become frustrated with being assigned tasks that don't interest them or draw on their strengths.

The following example illustrates how differences of organizational cultures may impact multicultural competence in interagency collaborations. Carmen Ruiz and Yvette Rogers are fictional department directors who have just met to discuss how their organizations might collaborate in providing FDC training for their front-line family workers. Each "cloud" describes each woman's thinking about how the collaboration might proceed, based on their first meeting.

What Carmen is thinking....

Yvette seems like an enthusiastic collaborator. We haven't worked with their agency before. She's eager to get things going and work out the "kinks" as we go. We don't work that way here. I need to present this at the next department meeting for approval before submitting to Ms. Erickson, the comptroller. Supervisors are interested, but I don't know how workers feel about this step. Then I need to check the "regs" and talk to union reps for any conflicts involving exempt and non-exempt workers. She's expecting more than our department can deliver in a short period of time...

What Yvette is thinking...

You can tell Carmen really knows her stuff. She's very professional and knowledgeable about what we need to do. I thought we were ready to get things started, but there seems to be a lot of people that she needs to get approval from first. We don't have all the details worked out, but my Executive Director is counting on me to get a training going in the next few months. My supervisors and workers are ready to start tomorrow. Jose, one of our other directors, has worked on a project like this before. Maybe I should ask him for help on how to handle this...

This vignette of Carmen's and Yvette's first impressions show well-defined differences between their organizational cultures. To explore some basic differences between organizational cultures, we'll use this illustration to compare four characteristics: organizational structure, leadership philosophy, formal and informal learning, and social norms.

Organizational structure

Organizational structure reveals the pattern of interrelationships among people and responsibilities in the organization. These structures are often described as either "flat" (i.e., the organizational chart depicts a structure that's more horizontal than vertical, indicating that authority, responsibility, and decision-making power are spread more equally across all the positions and among staff members who hold them; or "hierarchical" (i.e., more vertical than horizontal, indicating that authority, responsibility, and decision-making power are concentrated in the relatively small number of positions "at the top" and the relatively few staff who hold them). In the vignette, Carmen's description of her organization appears to be hierarchical and "top down" in structure, while Yvette's description of her organization appears to be "flatter" and somewhat entrepreneurial in structure.

Leadership philosophies

Organizations may also lean toward one of three *leadership philosophies*:

- Authoritarian (leaders-as-experts)
- *Laissez-faire* ("hands off")
- Democratic (everyone has a say)

In the vignette, Carmen's organization exhibits an authoritarian leadership philosophy within a hierarchical structure. Yvette's agency exhibits a combination of *laissez-faire* and democratic leadership philosophies within a "flat" structure.

Formal and informal learning

Formal and informal learning describes how leaders and workers gain knowledge to do their jobs competently. Formal learning is accomplished through a structured activity such as employee orientation; informal learning may be accomplished through chats "around the water cooler." Leaders and supervisors need to provide balanced opportunities for staff members to learn formally and informally in the organization.

In the vignette, Carmen's thinking revealed knowledge gained through formal learning—direct organizational experience and training in project management. Yvette decided to use an informal learning opportunity in her organization by asking an experienced colleague for advice faced with the realization that the project may not begin within her anticipated timeframe.

Organizational norms

Organizational norms are the accepted patterns of interaction and behavior that members use to relate to one another in the organization. Norms can include standards such as: how much familiarity is permitted between staff and supervisors, when and where people address each other using job titles, how quickly people move from surname to first names, and what is acceptable attire for the office. In the vignette, Yvette is impressed, while somewhat confused by Carmen's professional and cautious attitude, perhaps because Yvette has more open communication and access to her administrator.

Here are some ways to develop and build multicultural competence when working in interagency collaborations with different organizational cultures:

- When planning or starting a new collaboration or partnership, think about the potential differences in structure, leadership, learning, and social norms among the organizational cultures.

- Early in the collaboration, provide some time for supervisors and staff members from each agency to get to know each other in formal and informal settings.

- Establish guidelines and procedures about disseminating routine communication to partners—routines including what information is communicated to whom by whom, and how and when it's shared.

- If conflict surrounding differences in organizational cultures arises, use the information on resolving conflict in Chapter 4 to work toward creative solutions.

An interagency collaboration is much like the experience of any two partners interested in cultivating a long-term relationship. An interest in collaboration usually develops over time; through intermittent contact, partners begin to share ideas and realize there's common ground. As time goes by, they may decide to sustain their "friendship" by seeking funding or working together on a funding opportunity when it comes along. If there's just the right mix of strengths, services, and supports; a good plan; and a little luck, a project may be funded and the collaboration can begin.

At the beginning of an interagency collaboration, partners usually spend time deciding who will handle what duties and tasks, thus building the relationship. They invest time and energy to find a comfortable "fit" in their respective roles and to get the collaboration off to a good start. Then, as the collaboration passes beyond the initial phase, partners may become too busy to keep in touch. They plan to get together to talk about how things are going, but then have to postpone meetings when more pressing issues arise. Partners once eager to work together begin to feel "out of the loop." The problem is that the "loop" was never created from the beginning!

Here are some suggestions for keeping interagency partners in the communication-feedback loop:

- *Build information-sharing procedures into the routine activities required of the collaboration.* Leaders often spend too much time condensing large amounts of information into summary reports. Instead of reviewing all the monthly activity forms of every worker and then preparing a summary report, help workers design an activity form that gathers only the information specific to the collaboration. Take a few minutes now, or at a time when you're not stressed, to think systemically about what types of information you receive on a regular basis. If workers submit weekly activity reports but you don't get to read them until a week after you receive them, then you may not require such detailed information.

- If your agency uses family development plans that you review on a periodic basis, consider meeting with workers to discuss how to best capture the outcomes. If you decide that you can stay well informed by getting information less often and in a different format, discuss your ideas with workers or supervisors who provide that information, and get their feedback.

- Celebrate accomplishments together with families, workers, colleagues, funders, and others who have supported the collaboration. Being together, in the presence of those who both supported and benefited from the collaboration's outcomes, sends the message that all partners acknowledge and appreciate that support.

An example of empowerment-based interagency collaboration

Do you dream of the day when families have access to services they need, but which aren't currently available in your community? Do you envision that your agency could develop new and innovative programs without having to compete with other service partners for the same funding?

The Institute for Human Services, located in Bath, NY is a nonprofit management support organization founded in 1984. It provides support by continuously monitoring and researching management issues and trends in the local, state, and national nonprofit environment. It identifies regional needs, assets, and opportunities, communicating relevant information to member agencies, who pay a nominal membership fee.

One of its services is sponsoring the Southern Tier Non-Profit Executive Directors group, an opportunity for leaders to meet with their peers to share ideas, concerns, and opportunities. It also provides education and professional development that fosters networking and knowledge sharing. A forum such as this facilitates communication that often leads to interagency collaboration.

Another service the Institute provides is Resource Development. In today's changing environment, agencies often struggle to maintain critical services with almost daily threats of funding cuts. IHS Project Planning and Resource Development researches public and private funding sources and assists with the planning and writing of grant proposals that focus on collaborative efforts. It doesn't replace agency-based program development and grant writing, but rather focuses on larger collaborative projects that fill a critical need that individual agencies cannot meet themselves.

Early on, the Institute believed that incorporating a family development approach was key to transforming interagency collaboration in their region. A former Institute resource developer said, "Agencies providing services to families now use the family development model in interagency collaborative programs. Using this model, families have also become a part of the planning and design process."

At planning meetings, one of the first questions asked when a request for proposal (RFP) is presented is, "Can we do this collaboratively?" Here are some guidelines to help determine whether the timing is right for your agency and community:

- Reflect on your agency and community's capacity to work in the open and supportive climate required for interagency collaboration.
- Discuss with frontline staff what services and programs are currently working to identify and strengthen existing partnerships and coalitions.
- Look at trends in your community's resources, strengths, and needs, and use that knowledge to develop plans and goals.
- Discuss issues surrounding funding and territoriality in ways that help agencies balance the desire to collaborate with the need to serve their missions independently.

For more information about the Institute for Human Services, contact them at (607)776-9467, or visit the Institute's website at http://www.ihsnet.org.

Creating a new organizational culture using the family development approach

Creating a new organizational culture is hardest when the new culture is seen as counter to the established structure, relationships, norms, and image of the organization. In *Reframing Organizations: Artistry, Choice and Leadership*,[60] Lee Bolman and Terrence Deal describe the following components of the process of creating a new organizational culture:

- *Learning,* or developing individual and team skills to operate in a new culture
- *Realigning* relationships, visions, and goals around new outcomes
- *Negotiating* change from the basis of empowerment rather than authority
- *Reframing* outdated organizational stories, symbols, and assumptions in ways that provide a transition as old attachments are replaced with new ones

To this model, we add one more component we believe is crucial to creating a new organizational culture:

- *Reflecting*, or recognizing and cultivating the capacities of leaders, supervisors, and staff members who bring individual and collective creativity, intuition, flexibility, and mindfulness to their work

Supervision and leadership in today's society presents a challenge to create a new organizational culture—the "empowered workplace"—characterized by shared power, self-empowerment, empowerment-based leadership, and multicultural sensitivity. The following graphic illustrates how the components of creating a new organizational culture align to create a new Family Development Leadership Model.

The Family Development Leadership Model

Leading an Empowered Workplace
(*Learning*)
Empowerment-based training
Shared power
Understanding the family
development process for staff
Recognizing strengths and natural
assets of staff and the organization

Workplace Inclusiveness
(*Reframing*)
Respect for individual and collective
cultures
Promoting cultural competence and
cultural humility
Developing multicultural competence
in interagency collaborations
Creating a new organizational culture
using the family development model

The Empowered Supervisor and Leader

**Transforming Your Workplace
through Empowerment-Based
Leadership**
(*Realigning*)
Empowering, compassionate support
Aligning vision with mission
Building capacity for transformation
Talking the talk, walking the walk
Outcomes-based assessment and
collaboration

Supervising with Skill and Heart
(*Negotiating*)
Bifocal and peripheral vision
Developing workplace
relationships
Understanding group dynamics
Handling workplace stress and
conflict
Negotiating using the family
development model
Creative facilitation

**Leadership and Self-
Empowerment**
(*Reflecting*)
Principles of empowerment-
based leadership
Developing a personal vision
Effective leadership and
supervision
Mindfulness-based stress
reduction
Personal health and wellness

You already know that the steps of the family development process do not always follow a predictable pattern in a precise order. The same will hold true during the process of changing your organizational culture. This framework brings together the component parts to help you think about creating an empowerment-based organizational culture using the family development model.

Your organization already has natural assets and strengths. When all members of your organization and community are welcome to bring their natural assets and strengths forth in creating a new "empowered workplace," your organization will transform from simply being the "sum" of its parts, to realizing the unlimited potential of the whole. Let this potential encourage and continue to inspire you.

The process of organizational transformation shares many similarities with the journey of personal growth and development. We feel this passage from T. S. Eliot's "Little Gidding" reveals an insightful glimpse into the process of personal and organizational transformation in a simple and perceptive way:

> *We shall not cease from exploration*
> *And the end of our exploring*
> *Will be to arrive where we started*
> *And know the place for the first time.*

We wish you clear paths and helpful guides on your journey!

---

[47] This definition of multiculturalism was developed by Nathan Glazer in *We Are All Multiculturalists Now*, (Cambridge, MA: Harvard University Press, 1997).

[48] Nathan Glazer, *We Are All Multiculturalists Now* (Cambridge, MA: Harvard University Press, 1997).

[49] M. Tervalon and M. Garcia, "Cultural Humility vs. Cultural Competence: A Critical Distinction in Defining Physician Training Outcomes in Multicultural Education," *Journal of Health Care for the Poor and Underserved* 9, no. 2 (1998): 117-25.

[50] A. K. Kumagai and M. L. Lypson, "Beyond Cultural Competence, Social Justice, and Multicultural Education," *Academic Medicine* 84, no. 6 (2009): 782-87.

[51] Craig Moncho, "Cultural Humility Part II—Promoting Cultural Humility in the Workplace," *Social Work Practitioner*, Blogpost, (August 2013), http://www.thesocialworkpractitioner.com/2013/08/26/cultural-humility-part-ii-promoting-cultural-humility-in-the-workplace/.

[52] Milton Mayeroff, *On Caring* (New York: Harper and Row, 1971).

[53] Pew Research Center analysis of US Census Bureau data, 2019, http://www.pewresearch.org/fact-tank/2018/04/11/millenials-largest-generation-US-labor-force/.

[54] Jennifer Deal, *The Myth of Generational Differences in the Workplace*, American Management Association, blogpost (January 2019), http://www.amanet.org/articles/the-myth-of-generational-differences-in-the-workplace/.

[55] From http://www.mindtools.com.

[56] E. Schein, *Organizational Culture and Leadership* (San Francisco: Jossey-Bass, 1992).

[57] C. Argyris and D. Schon, *Organizational Learning II: Theory, Method and Practice* (Reading, MA: Addison-Wesley, 1996).

[58] U.S. Department of Labor, Women's Bureau (2016), http://www.dol.gov/wb/resources/breaking_down_wage_gap.pdf.

[59] Anne Fadiman, *The Spirit Catches You and You Fall Down* (New York: Noonday, 1997).

[60] Lee Bolman and Terrence Deal, *Reframing Organizations: Artistry, Choice and Leadership* (San Francisco: Jossey-Bass, 1997).

Chapter 5—Additional Resources

Books

Argyris, C., and D. Schon. *Organizational Learning II: Theory, Method, and Practice.* Reading, MA: Addison-Wesley, 1996.

Bennett, W. *The Index of Leading Cultural Indicators: American Society at the end of the Twentieth Century.* New York: Broadway, 1999.

Bolman, L., and T. Deal. *Reframing Organizations: Artistry, Choice, and Leadership.* San Francisco: Jossey-Bass, 1997.

Fadiman, Anne. *The Spirit Catches You and You Fall Down.* New York: Noonday, 1997.

Friedman, Stewart. *Total Leadership: Be a Better Leader, Have a Richer Life.* Cambridge, MA: Harvard University Press, 2014.

Glazer, Nathan. *We Are All Multiculturalists Now.* Cambridge, MA: Harvard University Press, 1997.

Loflin, Jones. *Always Growing: How to be a Stronger Leader in Any Season.* Mercer, PA: Elucidate Publishing, 2017.

Schein, E. *Organizational Culture and Leadership.* San Francisco: Jossey-Bass, 1992.

Stanier, Michael Bungay. *The Coaching Habit: Say less, Ask More & Change the Way You Lead Forever.* Toronto: Box of Crayons Press, 2016.

Articles

Gugel, M. "13 Characteristics of an Employee Empowered Culture." Blogpost, 2016. https://www.goco.io/blog/13-characteristics-employee-empowered-culture/.

Jartese. "8 Differences Between Traditional and Collaborative Leaders." Blogpost, 2013. https://blog.innocentive.com/2013/11/21/8-differences-between-traditional-and-collaborative-leaders.

Katz, J. H., and F. A. Miller. "Conscious Actions for Inclusion: A Common Language to Drive Uncommon Results." 2016. https://static1.squarespace.com/static/56b3ef5a20c647ed98996880/t/56f2c2cb4c2f85f9090ea7e8/1458750168176/Concious+Actions+for+Inclusion+AR.pdf.

Waters, A., and L. Asbill. "Reflections on Cultural Humility." American Psychological Association, 2013. http://www.apa.org/pi/families/resources/newsletter/2013/08/cultural-humility.aspx.

Ideas for Independent Learning Projects

Following are suggestions for independent learning projects to help you practice or reflect on inclusiveness, cultural sensitivity and facilitating organizational transformation. *We encourage you to develop your own independent learning projects that are relevant to your workplace or make modifications to the ones listed below to create a meaningful and manageable plan.*

- Consult the Institute for Human Services' website (www.ihsnet.org) to learn more about their services. Discuss the information and concept with another leader from an interagency collaboration in your area. Schedule or attend an interagency meeting to discuss ways that family-serving organizations can collaborate more effectively. Write a reflection on your experience, and describe ways that your organization will continue efforts and enhance interagency collaboration in your community.

- Explore aspects of your culture from the perspective of topics presented in the chapter: family or native folklore, historical events or eras, elements of your own cultural identity, customs and traditions, and your viewpoint on the movement toward a multicultural society. Complete the "Who am I?" exercise (either version). Write a reflection that incorporates what you've learned and that describes the origins, elements, and evolution of your culture and cultural identity.

- Identify an aspect of an individual or collective culture about which you want to increase your competence. Gather information from books, videos, the Internet and other sources about that cultural aspect. Interview a member of that cultural group to verify and enhance what you've learned through other sources. Write a reflection about what you learned through the entire experience and what you might do differently as a result.

- Learn more about your agency's organizational culture. Complete the assessment of basic elements of organizational culture presented in this chapter. Arrange for a colleague from another organization to complete the same assessment to get another view of your agency's organizational culture. Write a reflection describing the organization's structure, norms, relationships, and image. Describe one "organizational assumption" embedded in your agency and describe how it promotes or hinders empowerment-based approaches to working with families or collaborators.

- Learn more about another agency's organizational culture. Use the *Organizational Culture Interview Guide* to facilitate an interview with a staff member from another organization of your choice. Ask for a copy of the agency's latest brochure or newsletter. Write a reflection describing aspects of that agency's organizational culture and its strengths as a service provider in your community. Identify ways your agency could increase its multicultural organizational competence and support for families by developing or strengthening its relationship with this agency.

Organizational culture interview guide

Directions: Use these questions as a guide in facilitating a conversation with an interagency colleague or staff member about their agency's organizational culture. Ask for a copy of an agency brochure or recent newsletter to help supplement information you'd like to learn.

1. Please describe your agency as if I were someone new to our community. What does your agency do? Whom does it serve? What types of service(s) or products does it provide?

2. Could you give a brief history of how the agency got started? What geographic areas does the organization serve? How is it funded?

3. What are the agency's qualifications for entry-level employment? What types of positions does your agency have?

4. How does the agency operate administratively? Do you have an executive director, chief executive officer, board of directors, or advisory council?

5. How should an agency interested in collaborating with your organization make initial contact?

6. What type of leadership style do you think your organization has? (You may need to explain the basic differences between authoritarian, *laissez-faire*, and democratic styles.)

7. What types of professional development training are offered to workers, supervisors, and other staff members?

8. How does your agency learn about the needs of its families and decide to develop collaborations with other organizations in the community?

9. What are some of the customs of your organization with regard to:
   - Use of surnames and titles
   - Familiarity between supervisors and workers
   - "Unofficial" dress code

10. What should leaders from another agency know about your agency's culture to develop or strengthen their working relationship with your agency?

APPENDIX

- Independent Learning Project
- Leadership Empowerment Plan
- Family Development Plan
- The FDC Code of Ethics

Independent Learning Project

Name: _____ Chapter: _____

Description of independent learning project (include date, participants, and setting):

_____

_____

_____

_____

Reflection on this experience (attach other sheets, if necessary):

_____

_____

_____

_____

_____

_____

Reviewed with Peer Advisor: _____

Peer Advisor signature _____ Date _____

Peer Advisor reflection:

_____

_____

_____

_____

_____

Leader Signature/Date: _____

Leadership Facilitator Signature/Date: _____

Official National Family Development Credential Program/University of Connecticut

Leadership Empowerment Plan for _____

Today's date _____

Short-term goal:

_____

Steps leading to this goal

Steps you will take and when: *Steps your peer advisor will take and when:*

_____

_____

_____

Your personal assets and strengths

In your words: *In your peer advisor's words:*

_____

_____

_____

Concerns

In your words: *In your peer advisor's words:*

_____

_____

_____

Services and resources available (include names, addresses, phone numbers, etc.):

_____

Date, time, and place to review progress: _____

I will support _____'s plan to achieve this goal and agree to meet to review progress.

_____

Peer advisor's signature   Date

©2003–2019, Claire Forest

Family Development Credential® Program

Family Development Plan

(Include with the portfolio)

Directions

Family worker: Ask the family if they want to fill out the form or prefer you to complete. If you complete, be sure to use their words. If the family member wants you to do the writing, read out loud what you have written. Ask them for any corrections, and make the corrections they request on all the sections except "in the worker's words." Give a copy to the family member, and keep a copy in your file. Each of you should review the form before your next meeting, to make sure you've each taken the steps you agreed on. Begin your next meeting by reviewing the last plan.

- Family member's name (indicate preferred title: Ms., Mr., Miss, Mrs., etc.):

- Address:

- Phone(s) (note if home, work, or friends, etc.):

- Other family members involved in family development process (let family define whom they consider family members, please note ages and gender):

- Today's Date: [   ]   Worker's Name: [   ]

- Goal (in family member's words):

- Help family brainstorm possible steps leading to their goals:

- Help family choose steps to take (note date each will take place):

- Steps family will take and when   Progress/obstacle

- Steps Worker will take and when   Progress/obstacle

At your next meeting, note progress or obstacles to each step listed above:

- Family strengths and resources (in *family member's* words):

- Family strengths and resources (in *worker's* words):

- Concerns (in *family member's* words):

- Concerns (in *worker's* words):

- Services available (include details such as names, addresses, phone numbers, hours, etc.):

- Notes:

Family Signature

Date Reviewed

Worker Signature

Date Reviewed

NEXT MEETING DATE, TIME, PLACE: Click here to enter text.

If you cannot keep this appointment, please call:

At: By:

THANK YOU FOR YOUR COURTESY!

The FDC Code of Ethics

The FDC Code of Ethics was developed by Wojciech Konopka, M.S.W., in collaboration with the Cornell Empowering Families Project and statewide FDC instructors, portfolio advisors, and supporters. We encourage you to share and discuss the FDC Code of Ethics which follows, with everyone in your organization and to refer to it whenever your agency develops and implements agency-wide staff policies. Using the Code as a guide will help you and other leaders in your agency respect the individuality and value the collective contributions of all staff members as well as the family members you serve and support.

Introduction by Wojciech Konopka[61]

Ethics is defined as the systematic exploration of questions about how we should act in relation to others. Ethical dilemmas come in all shapes and sizes. Our task is to prevent and deal appropriately with ethical problems. The thoughtful study of ethics and FDC Code of Ethics can not only benefit one's professional interactions, but also all areas of one's life.

Why do we do, or not do, the "right thing?" Often it is because of an established rule or law, but without thoughtful reflection, our ethical decisions are too often based on our own moral judgments and standards, as well as our personal needs. As we study ethics we touch on conscience, our basic inner guidance system, and the consequences of our actions. Discussion of ethics is vital and can motivate us to reach for a higher standard of integrity in all areas of our life.

The development of our moral judgment is an ongoing and continuous process. Practical tools such as the FDC Code of Ethics can help us make the right ethical decisions. Following rules, laws, codes of conduct are all a part of living an ethical life, but the real strength comes in the principles that we internalize and integrate into our lives. When we do this, behaving in an ethical manner becomes automatic. A well-rounded life-long education in ethics considers character, conscience, courage, and other principles and traits that play a part in our decision-making process. Rules do not cover every situation. Life is full of gray areas.

The FDC Code of Ethics provides a reference for developing skills of ethical conduct. These principles can help us find direction in murky situations. As ethical people, what can we do when we find ourselves in a situation that presents an ethical dilemma? Often the "right thing" is obvious, but sometimes it is not easy to know if you have made the right choice or chosen the higher principle. The Code helps us consider our options, and refine our responses.

FDC Code of Ethics

FDC recognizes that many decisions required of those who work with families are of a moral and ethical nature. The FDC Code of Ethics gives guidelines for responsible behavior for resolving ethical dilemmas encountered by FDC workers, portfolio advisors, and trainers. The Code also establishes shared professional ideals and principles that affirm our commitment to strengthening families. The guidelines and principles are intended to provide a basis for conscientious decision making.

Section A: Families and ethics

Principle: *The goal of family development is best accomplished by ethical care and concern in helping families identify, set, and achieve initial goals of healthy self-reliance and interdependence with their communities.*

Family development professionals can support families in this process by:

- Developing strengths through collaboration and promotion of self-esteem

- Supporting family empowerment by helping families build upon their strengths and competencies
- Safeguarding confidentiality in working with families and treating all information with care
- Maintaining safe, healthy, nurturing, and mutually respectful relationships, and refraining from inappropriate physical, verbal, or sexual conduct with family members and co-workers
- Establishing relationships based on mutual trust and respect
- Respecting the dignity and valuing individual differences of all families and cultures, as well as their customs and beliefs
- Respectfully interrupting and handling oppressive behavior that is disrespectful, degrading, dangerous, exploitative, intimidating, psychologically damaging, or physically harmful toward others
- Recognizing and striving to eliminate practices that discriminate based on race, ethnicity, gender, class, family form, religion, physical and mental ability, age, and sexual orientation
- Reporting suspected abuse and neglect of children and adults to appropriate authorities.
- Enhancing their knowledge base, skills, and competencies to work effectively with others through continuing education and training

Section B: Ethics in the workplace

Principle: *All individuals and families have the right to confidentiality and privacy.*

Family development professionals protect this right by:

- Obtaining written permission to provide information to others and knowing the legal guidelines and procedures for sharing information based on situations of abuse, neglect, or in life-threatening situations
- Developing relationships that strictly avoid potential exploitation of others or using relationships for private advantage or personal gain
- Maintaining confidentiality regarding information shared in meetings regarding individuals, problematic work situations and personal information
- Respecting a families' right to have access to records and receive assistance in interpreting them

Section C: Workplace and community ethics

Principle: *Family development professionals and their organizations coordinate, cooperate, and collaborate with families, agencies and other helping systems to develop and offer services and support to families.*

Family development professionals and their organizations can support this principle by:

- Sharing resources and information with families, colleagues and other agencies as appropriate
- Reporting unethical or incompetent behavior only after direct informal efforts to resolve conflicts have failed
- Providing community with high-quality, culturally sensitive programs
- Recognizing the strengths and needs of families and communities and empower them through research, education, and advocacy
- Supporting policies that promote the empowerment of families and cooperating with other individuals and groups in these efforts

---

[61] Our thanks to Wojciech Konopka, M.S.W., for his leadership role in the development of the FDC Code of Ethics, and to the FDC facilitators, field advisors, and supporters who collaborated with him.